A Big Thank You to all those who never believed in me and never supported me through anything in my life....You All were my motivation and such a great inspiration in my life.

-EYE DON'T THROW SHADE, EYE SHED LIGHT-

This is no ordinary book. In matter of fact, this is not a book. These are thoughts in motion and different energies and vibrations dancing through the pages and absorbing in the reader's mind. When your mind is free, there is no direct guideline. There will be no chapters or page numbers as you continue to read, so just open your mind and just flow with it. There is no limit to what Eye say or anyone telling me that Eye shouldn't say a certain thing. You will be hit in every direction with a random, versatile, thought process. Open your mind and let me enter in.... Are you ready?

"It is better to be "STILL" rather than to be "Silent"..... (Well what are you saying Goldyn?)....Eye am saying that sometimes "Silence is violence"...We are silent on the outside to use as a mask to cover up what's going on in the inside...While we are silent with a quiet tongue, we are boiling inside with unbalanced emotions that we are trying to keep calm but in reality, it is eating and killing us slowly...

But 2 be "Still" means that we have mastered that self-control and while we face uneasy situations, we have enough peace and balance to wither the storm inside. Once the inside is right, then the outside will just flow with it..No matter what words you speak, you will remain "Still" rather than a "Silent Killer".

*How many of us are in rage inside about situations but remain in Silence...How many of us remain "Still" in the midst of chaos and turmoil, knowing that where there's a will, there's a way?

Many people always ask me..."Why do you do what you do?, You see how bad the condition of some of our people are, why keep trying? Then they say, "Stop trying to change the world because you cant." Then they say, you spend to much time being concerned about others....You Think you know everything."

So after Eye sit there and smile,... my answers to all their questions are...

Eye don't know why Eye do what Eye do.....when your highly elevated in your Chakras, the Spirit takes over....If Eye can change, so can others, and who am Eye to say that there is no hope for anyone particular. What Eye do is not time consuming because my visions, knowledge, wisdom & thoughts are already stored in my mind, body, & soul, so all Eye have to do is breathe them into existence unto any platform. Last but not least, If Eye can touch one person...If Eye can spark just one mind to influence them to change for the better, then Eye have helped changed the world....

Sometimes we are a prisoner of our own thoughts. Some trust their lower consciousness more than their higher consciousness. A weak person settles for negativity, not knowing that they are in control of their own reality. Distance yourselves from negative thinkers, stop absorbing & entertaining negative energy and low vibrations from others. Whatever kind input you put in, don't be surprised at the output that will return to you...

It is so much easier and less stressful for me when you keep it real and just be yourself rather than create this false image that's going to be stressful and time consuming to you. Eye never try to be a role model, Eye just prefer to be a REAL model....that way you cant let anyone down and they only can expect you to be you..

Eye get asked a lot of times, Do Eye believe in God or what religion Eye am. My thoughts on that is how can you truly Know, Love, & build your own connection with God when you are allowing people with money and power tell you how to Know, Love and build a connection with God?

The hardest question for themselves to answer is....Tell me who is God to you without using a handwritten religious book? Hint, You will find this answer within yourself. Stop repeating what people have taught and told you because you will eventually tell that lie or their experience to yourself and believe it, & then teach & program your kids the same lie. If you can't answer this, maybe you haven't really found God. By the way, Eye don't want to know your answer...that's something that's personal to you. Eye just want to see your LIGHT and then Eye will see the God in you and believe you.

-You will find, knowledge, Wisdom, Morals, & guides in these books...NOT GOD(The Most High).-

All the knowledge & compassion in the world would not change someone that doesn't want to be changed...It takes Wisdom to connect with someone's spirit to get inside the mind of an individual, to make them really evaluate themselves to become better.

"Knowledge is only the set foundation but it takes Wisdom to build others up and to bring forth action."

*Know The difference between knowledge and Wisdom or you will just be a person talking, thinking you know everything and have figured everything out.

"ALONE"
.......silent whispers of the ocean calming the spirits that are lost at sea....Alone.....Eye hear no yelling or crying, or do Eye see any dying...Eye feel peace and warmth, while the water keeps me dry from wet sorrows...Reality is false while dreams, fantasies, & fairy tales are very true....Ever wonder why the Sun still lights up the sky when the clouds are gray and it's raining too?...Alone...Eye cant believe my eyes...Eye see home..Eye see a beautiful place....Eye see their hands out to hug and welcome me, asking me where have Eye been....Eye see children laughing, playing and dancing....Eye see Men, Women, boys and girls smiling...Eye see the trees and flowers conversation while blowing in the wind...Eye see the animals of all kind roaming with no fear or anger, just embracing their habitats....Eye see no chains, & Eye see & feel no pain.....Alone...all of a sudden, Eye hear and see nothing...Eye can only feel the presence of this place..And then....but wait...All Eye can hear again is the silent whispers of the ocean calming the spirits that are lost at sea."

-Freedom of the Mind is a Peace of Mind-

Eye think Eye have come to the point where Eye have found myself loving people more than they actually love themselves, ...and no matter how Eye try to show that Eye care for them, they take it as an attack to them where they feel they need to get defensive...No matter how positive and logical you be to a broken, emotional person, they will always find something negative about the message or the approach, just to remain comfortable in denial of their errors.

Sometimes people in your life that's close to you will tell you that your a loser, no good and that you will never amount to anything...and we will start to believe them... Then you will get to a point where you expect to screw up or you expect to fail in everything you do...but if we want to win, we have to let that conscious go, let those people go and forgive them and move on because you are only giving them the power that they do not deserve. Believe in yourself and win despite of the Father or Mother or any kind of Love and support you never had from your love ones...Forgive them and move on....Eye just did...Sometimes it takes a little time to build up that confidence...so surround yourself with positive and supportive people.

Eye have stopped casting my pearls unto the swine because everyone doesn't want to elevate because many are very afraid of heights.

It may be some stuff Eye see or read that's gonna make it hard to smile. Eye have to learn to handle constructive criticism. Eye have to learn to control my emotion..You have to take in the bad as well as the good..Eye rather hurt you with the Truth, than comfort you with lies, just so your feelings won't get hurt..You have to know who you really are...You have to know your worth and true purpose...You have to know how beautiful & strong you are.

(Eye Have Seen Many Women Naked)

"You think you've seen her naked
because she took her clothes off?
Tell me about her dreams. Tell me
what breaks her heart. What is she
passionate about, and what makes
her cry? Tell me about her childhood.
Better yet, tell me one story about
her that you're not in.
You've seen her skin, and you've
touched her body.
But... you still know
as much about her as a book you
once found, but never got
around to opening."

"Nah, you haven't seen that woman naked before or even touched her skin. Maybe you touched her body but she never let you in. Did she cry when you entered her womb? Did her universe shake and quiver from the eruptions of her sexual volcanoes? Nah, you haven't seen that woman naked before. Do she feel so comfortable around you that she presents her natural self to you without the makeup and weave? Does she run to you with open arms just to be healed? Have you seen her before she was able to stand on her two feet? And last but not least, when you see her in a public place surrounded by many people, do you stop the time and make her look your way and stare at you so deeply that you melts her soul just because she knows that you are one of the few that really saw her naked? Now, she has exhale."

*Many Men have been in relationships with many women and still is, but never saw their woman truly naked.

Eye think to myself all the times that SOME Black Women are so broken that it is so obvious to see. They have no knowledge of self and they want to be everything else rather than A Black Melanin, African Nubian Queen. They carry themselves with a European standard. They hate their natural hair, she hates her skin tone, they hate their eyes....they hate their eye lashes... they hate they eyebrows..Eye they hate their bodies...they just hate the way they look because they are too busy trying to look like white women. They are so ashamed to show their natural self to the world, and also they hide behind a fake image.

They don't know or understand that they are spiritually connected to the Black Man but they will explore relationships with other races of people knowing that they will never truly love them..You will see and know this because she always will have a child by the Black Man...The Black Man have hurt them so much that they have giving up on love and themselves, so they became bitter, rebellious, & careless, while enduring a negative attitude..She became hurt & out of control, so she screams for attention..She desires to be wanted or love because she became so insecure with herself...So she reveals her body to the world so seductive, just to be seen while knowing that she really hates herself...She takes several pics of herself everyday trying to convince herself that she is beautiful. She then gives up her body to any man that flatters her just to fill that empty void inside...But that feeling doesn't last long, so she is on to the next.

    Now she lowers her standards for money and material things..If a Man doesn't have a lot of these things she is not interested..So she spends most of her life as a bitch and she would rather be called that, because Now, she has put a price on herself...

    Behind closed doors, she is hurting and dying inside and all she needs is a strong Black King to really, Eye mean really love her and to tell her she is beautiful...Also to love, honor, and protect her...A Man that will hug her so tightly that all her broken pieces will come together and be healed.. Once that Black Woman is healed and balanced, you will see the change in her..She will be less aggressive, less angry, and more understanding...She will finally slow down and humble herself...So, when you see these women out of control in person or on the internet, just know that these are broken and unbalanced women that needs to be fixed because they are hurting inside....Mostly because of us, the Black Man, who some of us have failed our women....Men, we have to step back up on the throne....Teach the Black Woman about her melanin skin...teach her about her 9ether hair...teach & show her that she is a Queen...show her she is God.."

    Eye don't thing anyone will ever prosper, succeed, or see their true purpose in life, if they are ashamed and afraid of their own reflection in the mirror. You can never run away from who you really are.

Something just popped up in my mind. Eye was always very afraid and cautious about having sex with multiple women. Let me tell you why. Eye found out about Sexual Transmitted Demons.

Sexual Transmitted Demons are more powerful and effective than any other disease..These are called Soul-ties..You connect with that person's spirit every time you enter the woman's womb or let a Man enter your womb...You take in all their energy and spiritual demons and emotions of being angry, bitter, evil, insecure, or whatever they may possess inside them.

We as a people have been so careless with sex..We treat it as a hobby or just fulfilling a need or sexual desire...Sex is more spiritual, than physical...Just look around at everyone and evaluate on how casual sex have done to our people..Why are our people so angry, out of control, insecure, no morals, bitter, and unstable? It is because we have all these other people's demons inside of us that we have gotten from multiple sex partners and we can't control them.....For an example, when a virgin looses their virginity...you will know because they will think and act differently because they are walking around with someone else spiritual demon inside of them..It's like a domino effect and some have more demons than others...So whoever you decide to have sex with, you are connecting with their demons and the demons from all the other partners they have had down the line, etc,etc...

Also when we create seeds with these people with these unstable demons, it is already effected the children spirit...and you will see it in their character.

Queens....Be careful who you let inside your womb...& Kings, be very careful on who womb you decide to enter...it might change your life...Don't let the pretty faces or sexy bodies deceive you and lower you into a destructive, spiritual temptation.

Hmm....Money is very tricky and will deceive you.

LIFE
OF MODERN PEOPLE

Eye will just leave this here and most people will not be able to dig this concept or the logic of this meme, because their too busy digging there own graves..But Eye will ask you this...How many people have you crossed, killed or hurt for money? How many sons and daughters have you neglected for money? How many self morals & life values have you given up for money? Whatever wrong you have done or doing now for money, you will feel that same pain that u caused others...

Not one penny have left this earth but a lot of people left and still is..The earth rotates for a reason...& money will always circulate over and over, so there's no need to chase it...So be careful when you make your next move."

CHECKMATE! GAME OVER!!

Eye have come to a point where Eye am not worried about anything because Eye know that there is a time for everything. Worrying is not preparation...though sometimes you may think it is. The next time your mind is occupied with worry, remember that worry doesn't prepare you for anything. Decide if there is something you can do that is productive about what you're worried about, or talk to someone for advice. Worry, in itself, blocks you, it's not productive.

Just look around and analyze certain things. A LOT of people are building bridges with people rather than A.R.K(one Act of Random Kindness)....People are doing things for others just to make others feel like they need them or to keep them in debt to them...These favors are not done from the heart anymore but rather out of a business deal...That's why so many people fall out over money and things they could not pay back..They use the term burning bridges...The question is...Do we really want to help these people? If you are respecting something in return when u help someone, it's best for you to not help them at all...Maybe some of the people out there will still be friends and families would be closer if we built an A.R.K. rather than bridges with one another.

Back to these relationships that Eye see that has everyone stressing and has gotten them to a point where they can't even focus or think straight. Listen closely...Eye am about to give you the game...Those who are in relationships or whatever the case may be...If you are the one who is insecure or always worried about someone cheating on you, you need to stop. Jealous & envy is a dangerous thing and also bad for your health. If that person is with you, their with you, just do what you suppose to be doing. You see, a lot of you are not doing what your suppose to be doing and that's why you get so insecure when your partner's attention goes somewhere else. But Peep this, a person is going to cheat regardless if you nag & spy on that person or not. It's nothing you can do about it. You just have to know who you are with and hopefully their the right one. Have confidence in yourself and your relationship because all that worrying and stressing about other people trying to steal your partner is irrelevant. People are going always admire and find the person you with attractive no matter where you go. It's totally different when someone is disrespecting you purposely trying to steal what you got...But don't be so much worried about who want the person that you are with...just take care of your business. Your relationships will be so

much less stressful, trust me. Insecurities & jealousy destroys relationships and pushes your partner away mentally & physically. That fire you have will burn out & your relationship will become like a prison, dull & boring.
*How can a person make someone be faithful when they don't want to? That's not realistic. You will only stress yourself into having a nervous breakdown or having a heart-attack trying to do that. Stress causes you to age quickly.

-Eye am going to put this out into the Universe and maybe someone will grasp this & it will be released from my mind.-

"Sometimes Eye feel that Eye am all alone in this World. Eye am giving and giving but never receiving from those who receive. Eye stay the same positive way to everyone despite if they like me or not. It seems that people will change on you when you are not giving them what they expect of you or acting like they expect you to act....If eye stay idle, no one will ask me how am Eye doing or do Eye need anything? Or they won't even just surprised me with a caring gesture. Eye have to always be the One to make the first move towards everyone. Everyone is stuck in their own selfish ways. Its like give me, give me...make me feel good or entertain me....If not, f*ck you, Eye have no need for you. That is not a healthy relationship to be in with friends or family.

    This does not make me weak but this makes me so strong & dangerous that Eye block everything out and become hard as a brick. Eye don't want to get to a point where Eye will isolate myself from everyone because Eye did it when Eye was a teenager for 2yrs straight. My positive character will never change but my surroundings definitely will. Eye will not force anything anymore, Eye will just let things flow and let people show me who they really are.

    Eye needed to talk to God, so Eye looked in the mirror within myself and began conversing. Eye bless the paper with my pen and emotions, because the paper never interrupts me and the paper is always humble enough to listen. No one knows what really goes on inside of my head, no one. Eye don't even think Eye know how to hurt anymore because Eye don't know how to take in or absorb negative energy.

All Eye can do is Love you the way Eye know how and Eye expect you to Love me the way you know how. Then the Universe shall balance itself.

So tell me you Love me, even though Eye know you don't Love me. Too much valuable time is wasting when death is around the corner.

As people get older they tend to judge more and they think they deserve to look down on younger folks. Well Eye say this, "Eye am a voice for the Youth who are looked down on and talked badly about. For the older generation or anyone that feel that we are hopeless is a disgrace to our people. We are young but we have heart. Some of our Youth only know what they see and they live in a concrete jungle, trying to break free. How can we lift ourselves up when you keep tearing us down with your foot on our necks? Why are you so afraid of us. We are what you use to be. Love us & guide us. If not, we will do it ourselves and Brothers like me will have to step up and be like a father figure & brother to our Youth. Eye will put myself in there shoes and shed the same blood and feel the same scars they feel. My people are beautiful & every flower can grow and be seen if the pile of trash is push aside. They say a rose can grow from concrete, but we plan on planting a whole garden. All we want you to do is listen to us and understand how we feel and why we act this way. Our innocence is still in us and it is covered up with neglect from our own elders & parents. Don't be afraid of us, just Love us, be a Light, so that we may see the way & the prodigal son & daughter will return home. We are too beautiful for you to give up on us. We all need Love and for someone to actually care for us. If you haven't took time out your so-called busy lives & tried to uplift us, don't u dare look down on us and talk negative about us. Come to the hood sometimes and see how we live and the few options we are given to survive. How can you be afraid of your own people. That's like looking in the mirror and being afraid of yourselves. We all go through stepping stones in life. So don't throw stones if you live in a glass house."

"Every time you awaken in the morning is a new day, and a new mind set..If you want to be mentally free, just make that choice and break those chains..Stay motivated and positive in everything you do and remember, no one owes you nothing. If you want it, you go get it..."

When Eye alone, Eye am always thinking about changing the world. When Eye say that we can change the world, Eye am meaning that we have the power to change our own world and spark the minds of others to have the desire to do the same. The choice is yours.

Always Remember that there will never be total Peace on earth and that is something that you should never pray for or desire because there will always be a balance of good and evil. The only true Peace that you will find is the Peace within yourself and that is what you should desire, pray, meditate, and strive for. Most people care more & put more effort towards the image they portray rather than the actions they display.

Why is it so easy to take what you have for granted and be chronically dissatisfied? But Eye think by focusing on what blessings you have can transform your mind and your life, ya dig. It is so easy to be caught up in feeling a sense of lack, encouraged by a culture that says that you never have enough and you are never good enough. Sometimes Eye find myself focused on that new car, a better relationship or even a different place to live as the key to making me a happier person. But now Eye know you by seeing my glass half-empty all the time makes my life seem miserable. Always looking for the future means you aren't really present in the life you have right now. By meditating on gratitude on a daily basis, you will reduce your dissatisfaction and increase your contentment with the life you have. Happiness, you will discover, is ultimately a state of mind.

When the road of hard times & tribulations seems so long, and it seems that it will never end, you must keep walking forward. Along your journey, you will stumble or may even fall down, but make sure you get back up...Sometimes it will feel like you are drowning from all the pain and sorrow in your life and that road that your walking down, will get flooded. If that happens, it's okay to lay down and stretch forward through the flood and swim through it..

Dark skies and rain falls are only temporary. If you can survive the flood, then you will blossom in the sunlight.

Eye know some of you are reading and you are wondering why the hell is he keep spelling the word Eye instead of I. Finally Eye will explain to the World why Eye use Eye instead of I when Eye type or write.

Eye use Eye because Eye am no longer standing alone or in darkness. All of my eyes are open to obtain and also give out knowledge. The Word I stands alone and it is without stability with no letters on each of its side. I has no meaning or cant produce life alone for me to use the letter I to represent myself. The letter I causes division & separation of self and from the people. There are 3 letters in Eye and it Represents the Father, Mother, & the Son. So Eye accept the Holy Trinity. Also Eye

Represents the Pineal Gland to inform the World that mine is decalcified & open. When Eye use Eye. Eye am speaking for the Trinity, my Ancestors, & those who are United with me in spirit. So Eye become a force, a powerful energy of vibration when Eye speak or write. That is that feeling that you cannot explain. That is that force that cannot keep you away. By me using Eye, it represents that Eye innerstand & overstand the reality of things.

*So Eye hope you dig what Eye am saying.

"If only our eyes saw souls instead of bodies how very different our ideals of beauty would be."

-WE FEEL BEFORE WE SEE-

Vibes & Energies are very important and very powerful. Sometimes you will just connect & feel comfortable opening up with a person and you cant even figure out why. When your vibrating, your vibrating & others will just feel it.

If I choose you, it won't be because you "look" good to me physically.. It will be because you "feel" good to me spiritually.

"The more you desire, the easier you will fall in love. The more you love, the less you will desire. So never desire to fall in love because love has no desire. It is already planted there, waiting to be nurtured and taken care of for it to grow. Love is a growing blossoming flower and desires are nothing but fresh fruit that needs to be picked and eaten before they rot, then its gone."

Not worrying about the negative things people say will bring you so much peace, but when you worry about the negative things people say and entertain it....that will only bring you stress and you will absorb that negative energy inside of you. No matter how much Truth you speak, some people will never get it or innerstand what your saying because their mind is too polluted and they are just not there yet in consciousness.

If Eye am not feeling you at the moment, Eye am not feeling you. Eye don't know how to pretend well and Eye am very outspoken (real). Don't get it twisted, Eye don't hate any human on this earth, it's just that it is certain people that Eye rather not being around to absorb their energies and soul ties. So never think Eye am acting funny when Eye just want to be alone at times or hang around people that are vibrating on the same frequency as Eye.
Eye know that their are many who feel the same as Eye do, We are One.

Old Soul

1# You tend to be a solitary loner.

Because old souls are disinterested in the pursuits and interests of the people in their age groups, they find it dissatisfying to make friends with people they find it hard to relate to.
 The result is ... old souls tend to find themselves alone a lot of the time.
People just don't cut it for them.

"Eye guess Eye am a old soul"

When you keep yourself in a box, your mindset will never change. My people, your going to have to start socializing with people that don't look and talk like you. If you don't, you will never innerstand anything or grow mentally. Sometimes real friends are more important than your own family members and they will show you way more love and concern. Anyone can treat you bad, family or not.

Eye have many friends of different races and cultures. It's all about Respect. Eye Respect who they are and they respect who Eye am (Solidarity). You don't have to be ashamed of who you are or pretend to be something your not in front of real friends. Love, Hate, Loyalty, Trust, & Respect stands alone and it is all different from one another.

Notice how most of these people in these Religions, Pro Black groups, and other boxed organizations talk...they all sound & think the same and they are so predictable. Trust me, you will learn a lot from different kinds of people...Eye have....then you will see how truly beautiful the world really is. Real friends are the family that you choose for yourself. Freedom of the Mind is a Peace of Mind.

"A comfort zone is a beautiful place but nothing never grows there."

Eye am mature enough to wish the best for people that Eye no longer talk with and mature enough to mean it. This is what you tell those people when they say you have changed or acting funny.

"Eye don't hate you, it's just that we were going in two different directions. Eye was ready to live and you was willing to die. Eye was ready to wake up and you was too comfortable sleeping. Eye wanted to walk with the Giants but rather you chose to stay crawling with the ants. This world is too big for me to stay

idle in a box with you, having the same mindset and outlook on life..."
*Love ones and true friends encourages you and ride with you to higher elevations in life, not those who are afraid of heights. Enjoy the new transition in your lives..

    Eye think about this a lot. The only way you will find out who truly care for you is when you are done stimulating them and they are still there. Okay, 85% of the people you meet in your life (friends & Family), do not really care about you. They will say they do and butter you up with pretty words, but their actions will never add up to what they say. The attention they give you is only because you entertain them or they have some type of agenda. But once they find you not so entertaining, they are on to the next person. Most people only care about themselves and nothing else. That day that you find yourself down and out or in a life and death situation, you will see the TRUTH and innerstand what Eye am saying completely and realize that there is no one there but you.

    Be thankful for people like me, because Eye am real enough to actually tell you the reality of things regardless of how it may make you feel. Eye know some of you don't really care about me and some of you only follow me because Eye stimulate your mind...and that's fine...but what happens when Eye stop stimulating you? That is the question...Eye pay close attention to a lot of things that people don't think Eye pay attention to..Eye just remain in silence and in peace and Eye wait for you to love me.

    Don't force so much knowledge unto people where you forget how to engage with them. Sometimes you have to be a great listener to really innerstand how they think and where they are coming from. Then you can make a connection and build from there.

    "Keep your Mind, Body, & Soul balanced and everything will be alright."

This just came to mind whenever Eye am around lots of people and they are conversing with one another. Eye have realized that no matter what kind of positive, productivity that you decide to do, there will always be people that will find something negative to say about you. As long as you know your true agenda behind what you do, that is all that matter. Just take care of you, your family and the people you care about, and those who really care about you as well. Sometimes Eye hate when people talk negative and say hateful things about celebrities or well known people that they don't even know or never even met in person. These people are nothing but insecure, negative people with negative energy. It makes my stomach hurt.

Also by not worrying about the negative things people say will bring you so much peace, but when you worry about the negative things people say and entertain it, that will only bring you stress and you will absorb that negative energy inside of you.

No matter how much Truth you speak, some people will never get it or innerstand what your saying because their mind is too polluted and they are just not there yet in consciousness. The messenger can only only deliver the message to those who can't vibrate to the message. So never stress yourself out by saying things to people who can't hear or innerstand you.

Some things in this world are priceless. Love is priceless, Trust is Priceless, & Respect is priceless. Those 3 things cannot be bought by anyone.

Some things Eye do are priceless and the Love pays it all in return. Some people won't innerstand my work ethic and the drive that Eye have. They keep asking me why do Eye do what Eye do and why do Eye care so much? So Eye say, "Sometimes, you are what you are and you cannot fight it and a higher force elevates you to the next level. You will know that you are fulfilling your purpose because it will come so easy to you and nothing can bring you down or discourage you to stop. Every time Eye write or be in the act of embracing someone, the time stops and Eye control the time and change the World.

    You will always have that joy inside of you and will always look for the positive in things..You start to take pride in whatever you have. Anger, Revenge, & depression is non existence to you and a smile from a random beautiful person can brighten your whole day. When you have peace within, it is an unbelievable and extraordinary feeling inside that is burning with passion. The one bad thing about this is that it will trouble those around you that are not right within and they will be your energy drainers. Until that have that inner peace, you will always irritate or frustrate them just by being you. Eye don't expect anyone to really innerstand why Eye do what Eye do. Just know that Eye have found me and embraced the God within. No one can never take me out of my character. Eye am my biggest motivation. Eye wink at ignorance & let The Most High balance the rest. Eye just do my part, and that completes me. You help me by the change you make in you. It is hard for small minds to comprehend huge spirits. To be great, you have to be willing to be mocked, hated, and misunderstood.

-FREEDOM OF THE MIND, IS A PEACE OF MIND-

    It seems that the most powerful and effective feeling in this world is LOVE. What is more amazing than loving someone and having them love you back? Eye am talking about that real love that will love you through anything and it doesn't even matter who you are. This love can come from your spouse, a friend, your children, or even a relative. You haven't really lived unless you have experienced the feeling of real love. Lack of love effects your character, language, and the decision you make in your life. Only a fool will go through life saying they don't need love. That person is only hurting inside, screaming to be loved and it making them unbalanced mentally and spiritually.
    Real love from others come when you are being the real

you. It feels so good to be able to express how you really feel inside and not be concerned or worried about what others may think of you. A lot of people are so worried about what their family, co-workers, friends, religious groups, or even the one that they are with will say to them, and that's really pathetic that you are so afraid of being yourself. How can you have a peace of mind and you don't even have a freedom in the mind to ask questions and to think for yourself? Be you, love you, or no one else will.

     Eye evaluate a lot of things and it is so weird that some Men will love, fight, represent, protect, live and die for their neighborhood rather than putting that same effort and love for their own family or women. They must haven't noticed that most of their women are paying attention to their actions. These same Men might think that these women are playing hard to get or just being stuck up but the reality is that they just don't trust or respect them enough to build with. These women want Kings, not little boys. That's why most of these Men cannot find real Queens and they are left complaining about the same basic hood girls that they deal with on a daily basis. If they want change, then they must change their mindset, character, and actions.

     "Your either going to be inspired or intimidated by me."

     As my friend if you hear other people talking bad about me; either you check them or you just as fake as them. Elders use to tell me all the time to watch who Eye let get close to me, but Eye use to always brush it off. You see, Eye trust people to be what they show me until they show me until they have shown me differently as they reveal their true selves. Eye am very sincere and a people's person but when it comes to a point where you are talking bad about me or letting someone who doesn't really know me speak so harshly about me, then Eye will not trust you anymore. Eye will not feel comfortable around you. Eye do not hate you, Eye just don't prefer to be around you anymore. It's like loving someone from the distance.

Respect is really a big deal. Eye have moved on from a lot of so-called friends and family members who envied me, hated me, and did not want me to succeed. It doesn't really matter how long Eye have known you, if you are bad for my life and a threat to me or my love ones, then Eye must elevate pass you, especially if those people do not want to grow as an individual.

Maybe Eye have to face the reality that some people will not love or respect you the same as you do them. A lot of people hate discipline or constructive criticism of changing for the better. Maybe it is because it requires a physical work ethic and most are too lazy to bring forth that kind of action. Real friends and family encourages you to be better than what you are but your closest enemies will rather for you to remain the same, stuck in the same place. They hate when you outgrow them and you start thinking differently from them. When you are at peace & in love with yourself, it will be easy to move from these kind of people.

They may ask, "How do you know if someone you hang with is talking behind your back?"

The answer is that it is all about the eyes, body language and energies that you get from that person....and yes you will feel it and know.

-FREEDOM OF THE MIND IS A PEACE OF MIND-

THE ALPHA MALE

Alpha male is a man who is dominate and does not make excuses for his shortcomings or any situation he may find himself in. He takes responsibilities for his actions and knows how to take leadership in the home or any kind of social or professional environment. He knows how to pull his women right beside him and guide her rather than controlling her. There is a huge difference between guiding and controlling a person. The alpha male is all about building and he make sure his woman is building as well....any means necessary. Jealousy and envy is not apart of his characteristic. The alpha male is not a people pleaser. He always tells the Truth and knows how to stand on his own two feet. He's very intelligent and does favors without expecting a return.

A Beta male is the total opposite of the alpha male. They are afraid to stand up for anything. They are called "Yes Men", meaning they need a leader to lead them. They always do what they are told. They are trained to color within the lines and not say anything that could embarrass themselves or anyone else. They need approval from others at all time and will go out their way to please people like putting on a false image of themselves. They hate to be disliked by anyone so they lie often, especially to women. They let their women control them. They let the woman take lead in their relationships to avoid confrontations. They do favors for people just to expect something in return and they hold grudges and resent certain people who are stronger than they are like Alpha Males. Beta Male makes excuses for everything and always play the victim of why they are in the situation they are in.

Trust me, A woman can tell the difference between these two men. Most Men don't innerstand that the Woman will never respect them if they do not know how to take charge, be masculine, guide them, submit to their feminine ways, discipline them and to love them at the same time. That is what turns them on and keeps them loyal to you, even your female friends. Most of these women settle for beta males because majority of the Men are that and they know that they need a man in this life to make their life easier. Most of our women never experience a real alpha male because their fathers were beta males, so they think that alpha male will be hard to find. Alpha Men have to show these women what a real man is, regardless of how uncomfortable they get. Beta Males need to stop bowing down to these women and letting them change their character and role.

THE ALPHA FEMALE

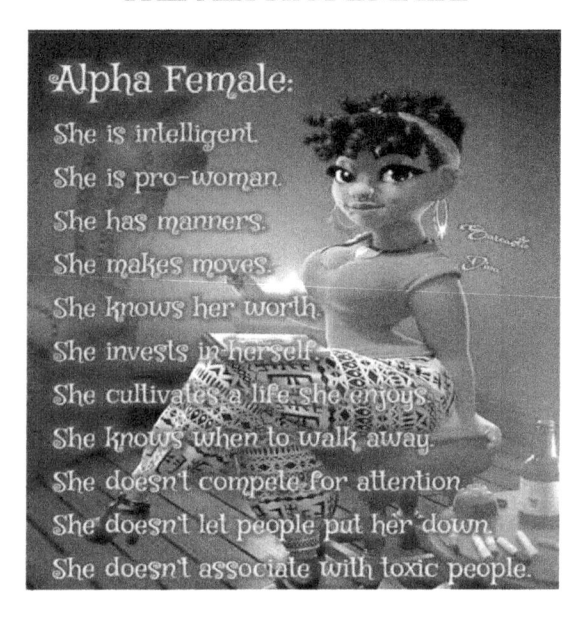

Alpha Female:
She is intelligent.
She is pro-woman.
She has manners.
She makes moves.
She knows her worth.
She invests in herself.
She cultivates a life she enjoys.
She knows when to walk away.
She doesn't compete for attention.
She doesn't let people put her down.
She doesn't associate with toxic people.

    The Alpha female is a strong, majestic female. She is very intimidating to those around her especially to weak Beta Males and Beta females. She is not afraid to ask for what she want and need. Her friends always rely on her and they love for her to be the center of attention of their group. An Alpha Male is her only goal and desire to have, that's why she stays single for a long periods of time, and those Beta Males will call her stuck up or full of herself & playing hard to get. She just knows what she want. The Alpha female is really not realistic to the Alpha Male because society has made it like a competition between the two. This is just a woman of confidence.

    The Beta female is totally opposite of the Alpha Female. She is very insecure and doesn't really know her true identity because she is always following trends of the world. She worries what others think of her and she plays relationship games with other beta males and will find herself alone while carrying his babies while letting him run all over her. She tends to find it hard growing up to become mature and self sufficient.

-FREEDOM OF THE MIND IS A PEACE OF MIND-

"Politics & Religion is only used by evil, egotistic individuals so they can lie, steal, gain riches, control, and have reasons to hate and kill certain people that they think they are better than."

Eye have been thinking a lot about this and it seems like we all are meant to be consumers of someone's product.

(strange but true)

1. The lawyer hopes you get in trouble
2. The doctor hopes you get sick
3. The police hopes you become a criminal
4. The teacher hopes you are born silly
5. The landlord hopes you don't build a house
6. The prostitute hopes you don't get married
7. The dentist hopes that your teeth decay
8. The mechanic hopes your car breaks down
9. The coffin-maker wants you dead
10. Only a thief wishes you prosperity in life!

Also, your religious leaders want you too suffer so you can depend on him and his God to comfort you, so you can be blinded by the deception that you see and only walk by a faith that is mythological. Faith means...to believe in something that can be true or not, but you believe it anyway with the hope of it being true. So you continue to train your mind of that same illusion.

"We're not meant to survive because this is a setup, but Eye know you fed...You gotta keep ya head..." -2pac

-Your struggle is always someone's hustle to come up.-

*Sorry....but this is the Reality that some are so afraid to accept. You would be at so much peace within yourself and in your life if you do. You also wouldn't be quick to get so offended and mad all the time. Never depend on anybody or anything. Don't wait for God, you be God until the Most High stop giving you the abilities and strength to overcome your obstacles.

"Learn, discover, and control your weakness before the World discovers it for you, to use it against you."

Quick thought! Some women in the Black Communities are becoming off balanced. Not just them, but women period. The government has given the Black Woman a false independent illusion & mediocre education and it has made their attitudes stuck up thinking they have real intelligence. Education does not define intelligence and it will show through their love lives and the choices they make with Men and the way they raise their children. Most black teens that are out of control are raised by single so-called educated & independent women with no intelligence of how to control their children or their own lives.

Eye hope my women of all races and cultures will stop falling for the trap and the set up that's creating a wedge between them and their men where they feel that you don't need a Man.

This thought just came to mind and Eye am tired of us making excuses. We as a people need to STOP blaming the so-called white man or Oppressors for everything we go through. Why do we give them so much power over our minds, body, & soul? We need to start taking responsibilities for ourselves and our actions. Don't be deceived into thinking that the white man runs and rule the world...that's what they want you to think. We all have the ability to rule and change our own world. The world is too big for a few men of greed to rule it. You cannot make people love you. Some never loved us and they will always show us that, so why try to be accepted by those people who don't want to love you?

Eye am not saying racism doesn't exist and that there are not any evil people in this world because they are.....but we can't put ourselves in a position and submit, and let them do anything to us. They only do what we let them do, so who fault is that? How can you call yourself a God, Goddess, King, or Queen if you are still blaming others and making excuses for your circumstances? If our Black groups are so real and powerful, why do some just sit back and let sh*t happen to your our people and do nothing? Who are they really working for?

They put drugs your community but you choose to use them and sale them to your own people. They put liquor stores on every corner but you choose to drink it and kill yourself from the inside out. They put poisonous restaurants in your city but you choose to stuff yourselves with that mess. They didn't make you hate yourself, you made the choice to go along with the plan. We are strong people and we are built that way and the world knows it. Whatever they throw at us, you take that sh*t and conquer it.....pick your head up and tell them, "what else you got for me". That's how you win....that's how you become successful. This is not their land, this is our land. Wherever we step foot on, it's ours, regardless of what they tell you. We cannot keep running away when things get hard.

If you are still making excuses and playing the blame game, then you are too weak for me to even associate with. You are no real Man or Woman because a Real Man & Woman make things happen without excuses. No one said it will be easy but only weak people take the easy way out. They are not destroying us, we are destroying us everyday, and just because we want to be entertained...the real joke is on us. All Eye see is us hating each other, lying to each other, killing each other, killing our unborn, abusing each other at jobs, breaking up our own homes, not loving our Men and Women, robbing each other, degrading ourselves, and disrespecting our own men and women. So who's to blame? WE ARE TOO BLAME!! It's time we take responsibility for our actions. Break this chain like some of us did. We don't make excuses...we hold our own...Eye control my life, no one else. Freedom of the Mind, Is a Peace of Mind.

      Yes, they did some awful and hurtful things to our people and that should actually tell us something of how important and powerful we are. Just imagine if the tables were turned and the sign was reversed outside of restaurants and restrooms....hmmm.

COLORED ONLY
No Whites Allowed

      Eye wonder how white people would've felt and reacted to something like this.....We educated everyone and we even shared our goods and resources. We just didn't know how evil some of people really were. Now that we are starting to love and embrace ourselves more, you want to say that we are all the same, now that u need us. But not to long ago, some white people didn't accept us and looked at us as differently like we wasn't human. Oh, how do you 4get...Remember, some of y'all never loved us.... now, you only only tolerate us because some of you have no choice. Certain whites always showed us how weak the white race are through racism and hatred. When will y'all grow up and strengthen up? Y'all are not privilege or superior to anyone. A lot of you guys ancestors were only thieves, manipulators, and murderers...and some still are.

      Some Caucasians made it this way and it will always be about color until y'all clean up this mess y'all made. We showed y'all nothing but love, and who you think taught y'all everything y'all know today? And the funny thing about it is that, we still don't hate you...but some of you still hate us...God's don't hate, we elevate..

*White people, be honest, how does this meme make you feel? Don't you all speak at once...y'all didn't mind when y'all did it to us and you are still doing it. We was never the problem, you guys were. You was the devil who roamed the earth seeking who you may devour. Be realistic, if we did what y'all did to us, y'all would never trust or love us. If we are the same then we will all look alike...stop the foolishness. Stop hating yourselves people. Love who you are, Love your differences. That is what makes the world so beautiful because we all all different. Don't get it twisted though...Good & Evil comes in all colors.

OK, enough of that. Its time to move on to another thought because people are gonna be people.

"How can we say we love God, whom we never seen, and hate our brothers and sisters, that we see everyday?"

You know what? Eye really hate the fact that sometimes when Eye am asleep and Eye try to awaken..... Eye can't because it feels like something is holding me down.

Eye know a lot of you have experienced this. This happens when you are sleeping and your brain wakes up but your body cannot move. You feel like someone is sitting on top of you trying to take your breathe away. Scientist and doctors will call this sleep paralysis. They will come up with all kinds of reasons why this happens, but the reality is that these are DEMONS & negative energy, that hangs around.

They normally look like Black shadows and they normally are spotted in the corners of your rooms. When your half sleep you can actually see these demons shadow moving across the room. They feed off fear. If you have animals in your homes they can spot them when they are awake. There is a saying of being careful who you let in your home because these demons need a host or a body to survive. So a person who has demons surrounding them can be released in your home. Also there is another saying of not going to bed angry or with any kind of negative thinking, because when you do that, you send off a signal to catch the demons attention. No matter what your beliefs are, you are not exempt from these demons finding you. If you Believe this or not, it doesn't matter because these demons believe in you. Demons can't hurt you without a physical body to work through.

*It's a lot more info to this but Eye will just give u the basics and also Eye don't feel like discussing this.

"A Wise Man can sometimes play the fool, but a Foolish Man can never play the Wise Man."

A lot of these people try to sound so profound and intelligent, that they don't even make any sense. It's like they read so many books that they will eventually confuse themselves. No matter how many books you read, it doesn't give you wisdom. Books can only give you certain knowledge of information that you need to open your mind, that's it. Everything starts within you...you cannot teach Spirituality...you can only teach religion, and history. If you are not right within before you read that book and grasp that knowledge, then that knowledge will be distorted inside of you and you will not gain Wisdom. You will be only a knowledge entertainer by only saying things that you read but have no innerstanding about how to use it in your day to day life. This is why you see people wrestling and debating with knowledge all the time and getting mad, because most of these people are not right within. They have no kind of Wisdom...These are smart, dumb people, and they have turned consciousness into a gang.

"The only true Peace in this world that we will have is the Peace within ourselves....Really living is knowing how to really live inside of your mind.. You can be whatever you want and travel wherever you desire....In our minds, everything is just the way we want it. Stop the time, because We control the time that doesn't really exist...Find Peace and you will be Peace in this world."

Eye will make this very clear and realistic. There is no such thing as eating 100% healthy. There will always be something that you are eating that your not suppose to eat...especially if you live here in America. So many people stress themselves out trying to find the perfect thing to eat, but cant. They even go vegan but fail to realize that even their vegetables and fruits are contaminated with chemicals.

Nothing, Eye mean nothing is healthy in the grocery stores. The air we breathe in holds chemicals, the water holds chemicals even when we try to purify it with fruits and vegetables.. Also in order to plant real fruits and vegetables, your soil have to be right and like Eye mentioned before the air outside that has chemicals are falling from the sky unto your harvest.

You might say, "How do we survive this?"....You have to keep an healthy balance in everything you eat, and stay away from dangerous meats that has powerful effects on you like pork and other meats that's rapidly causes obesity, worms, and other sickness. Stay away from fast food because it's fake and not real meat. You will know what's really bad for you after you eat it because you will feel lazy and drowsy....that means you should have eaten more lightly. Another thing is to meditate or bless what you eat.....remember you can't bless all things...but you have to control the mind and body. It's like being at a supernatural state to be able to heal yourself and your body will fight off the toxins you put in. Everyone's body is different and you have the common sense to balance it and not over due things. This is where your true Spirituality come into play to keep yourself healthy and not to be too over weight or too skinny.

Some might say, "well that's stupid"....but Eye have seen people eat all sorts of things and live a long healthy life in their late 90's....and their still living like my grandma and several righteous elders Eye know. Its all about a balance to not eat the same things constantly. Also you have to be elevated in the mind and spirit to control the body. Never get idle, always stay physically active to burn off the poison inside of your body. Once you get lazy and sit down, that poisonous food will start to effect you and how you think. It will also control your emotions.

*There's a lot of people telling you what to eat but 9 times out of 10, they don't know how to gain access to some of these foods that they tell you to eat, and they are eating unhealthy themselves behind closed doors.
*STRESS & LAZINESS KILLS YOU FASTER THAN THE FOOD YOU EAT.

"I now see with my 3rd Eye, now I have become an Eye, and Eye am no longer a victim of the blindness in my mind that was keeping my eyes from seeing."

Eye do a lot of analyzing on social media....in other words Eye feel the energy and emotions of people's post. This may sound a bit extreme and far fetch, but it's true. Many people on social media seek for Love & Attention. They do it because they lack the attention and Love in their physical day to day life. They tell social media that they don't need love or they post on how much they are such a loner, but the Reality is that, if you were such a loner, you wouldn't have social media. Eye see a lot of women doing things for attention....but Eye can see in their eyes and feel their energy that they are hurting and very lonely inside. They create this image for themselves and they are killing themselves even more because they have to keep these people pleased that they don't even know.

They settle for internet love and attention thinking that it's going to fulfill that empty void. Their Likes on their pages may boost their self-Esteem for the moment but it will go back down if their Likes get too low. Social media causes mental damage and pushes you away from reality. 95% of these women and men are not Revolutionaries or who they say they are, and they won't say the things in person they post on the net. Anyone can make a video talking to themselves rather than speaking live in front of a criticizing crowd that have the ability and opportunity to approach you face to face. Most people are fighting for attention when they should be fighting for their lives.

*Remember social media is just entertainment, a trend, and a popularity contest for most people where they can be whomever they choose to be. So enjoy the show....many sheep will me fooled but a Lion can seek out the cowards and imitators.

Waking Up

The hardest part is waking up. When your so comfortable sleeping and you know that you have to wake up, you get kind of frustrated and you feel so weak and tired that you just want to submit and go back to sleep. So, what do you do? You forced yourself to wake up and you nourish yourself with some breakfast and nutrition like oatmeal, grits, eggs, cereal, coffee and fruit or whatever you decide to put in your body. Meaning, you put these things in your system to function properly to uphold your awakening.

So what that being said....Always use this concept when it comes to waking up mentally and spiritually. A lot of us are still comfortable sleeping meaning we are too comfortable in our way of thinking and living and we will get very frustrated and angry when someone try to awaken us or motivate us to change for the better. But if you decide to awaken, remember you will need to keep adding that nutrition(fruit) to your mind to help you function properly. When Eye say nutrition and fruit, Eye mean fruits of knowledge that you seek and take in constantly to avoid going back to sleep. Once you are awaken, it will be very hard to go back to sleep. Always remember....THE HARDEST PART IS WAKING UP!!

"All Books were written by Men & Women to open the mind...not for us to believe every word and take everything literally. It's all a puzzle, and you must find the WISDOM to put the pieces together. Knowledge will not help you alone until you have the WISDOM to guide you, to put things into physical action."

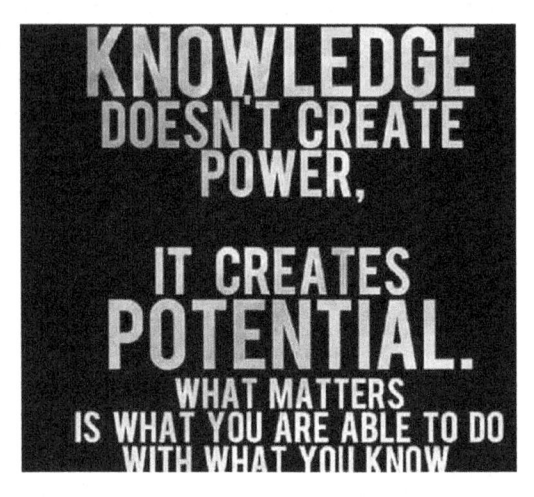

> **KNOWLEDGE DOESN'T CREATE POWER, IT CREATES POTENTIAL. WHAT MATTERS IS WHAT YOU ARE ABLE TO DO WITH WHAT YOU KNOW**

Read this carefully and try to innerstand this deeply inside of your soul. You have to learn to really Love & Live for yourself first in order for you try to Live & Love for someone else. Eye tend to hear a lot of people say that only live for their spouse or children, but we must remember that we also have our own lives to live and no one can live for us forever. We were all born to eventually spread our wings and fly in our own direction and take our own paths in life. No matter how hard it gets, never live your life through anyone because you might not like the direction that they are going in while using their own free-will.....and this will cause you stress and anxiety. Love and Embrace yourself and define your own destiny in order to manifest those other lives around you. You have one life to live, so you better make it count and always remember to seek your own purpose in life.

"Sometimes the blind eyes can see things that the eyes with sight can't see...and sometimes the deaf ears can hear what the sound ears can't."

Eye have notice that when you start doing certain things that no one innerstands, you become a threat to them for some odd reason. When this happens, it just tells me that Eye am actually doing me. One of my female friends told me that you tend to loose a lot, yet the Peace, Confidence, Love, Innerstanding, Power, Contentment and Oneness that you gain, cuts the attachments to those who's keeping you idle while bring you down.

"Learn more, See more. Listening is a skill....and a lot of people lack that skill."

"First, you must prove to yourself of how great you are before you try to prove it to the world." Eye let this statement sink into my brain all the time as a reminder of when Eye lack confidence or if Eye don't have the drive to keep pushing to accomplish my goals. Eye am not going to lie because sometimes Eye just don't feel like doing anything but relaxing and watching time fly. Then Eye have to catch myself in my idle moments and be like, "What the hell am Eye doing?" Sloth is a deadly position to be in. It's like you are taking your life for granted while others may be fighting just to live.

If Eye am at a 9 to 5 job, Eye will just be inside of my mind while working, constantly asking myself of why am Eye here. Eye know we all need money and we have to start from somewhere, but why does it feel so long and miserable? It's like Eye am surrounded by individuals who are satisfied by working for others their whole lives. It's like they have giving up on their dreams or maybe they have gotten too comfortable and they have convinced themselves that there is nothing better out there.

Concerning myself, Eye will never be satisfied working and retiring from someone else company. That moment when you give up on your dreams and stop supporting them, someone will hire you to support theirs.

"The heart must be broken for it to open up so it can influence the mind to do the same."

A quote by the late Medgar Evers really made a lot of

sense to me. He said, "Hate is a wasteful emotion. Most of the people you hate never know it and the others, just don't care."

Likewise as to being angry. If you plan to do nothing physical about the situation, all you doing is drawing more negative energy and lower vibrations to yourself. That's when you loose power, then your adversary gains control over you.... then your emotions starts to control your mind.

Concerning myself...when people try to make me angry, Eye laugh, because they only did what Eye expected them to do..It's very hard to gain control of my emotions.

Sometimes dealing with people is like playing chess. Its like you have to use certain strategies in life like this; "Some of the most loyal and dedicated people you can deal with are the people you've proven that you could destroy, but gave them a chance to redeem themselves. Leave even your adversary with their dignity, because if you don't, they will spend the rest of their life trying to destroy you.

Make an enemy into your friend and maybe they will see the value of being your friend. Make an enemy into an example and everyone will definitely see the value of being your friend.

*Your enemy if very tricky and can be anyone far from you or really close to you like your best friend, cousins, sister, brother, mother, father, or even your spouse..A wise person will never show an emotion of anger because they know once they show anger towards you, they become so predictable that they can be easily controlled and easily destroyed. #checkmate!!

Being mentally strong is a strength and if you know how to use this strength, it will be very beneficial to you. 12 easy steps you can build from to be mentally strong are.

1. Don't fear alone time.
2. Don't dwell on the past.
3. Don't feel that the world owes you.
4. Don't expect immediate results.
5. Don't worry about pleasing everyone.
6. Don't waste time feeling sorry for yourself.
7. Don't waste energy on things you cannot control.
8. Don't let others influence you to have negative emotions.
9. Don't resent on others people success.
10. Don't shy away from responsibilities.
11. Don't give up after the first failure.
12. Don't fear taking calculated risks.

Your real self is hidden within you and is fighting everyday to be revealed to the world. The real self is dangerous. Dangerous for the established religions across the world, dangerous for the state, dangerous for the crowd, dangerous for the common traditions, because once a person knows their real self, they become an individual.

That person no longer belongs to a group; they will not be superstitious, and they can never be exploited. That person can never be led like cattle and cannot be ordered or commanded. They will live accordingly to their Light and will live from their own inner self. Then their life will become beautiful.

"When Eye am alone, Eye tend to get lost in my mind."

"What if life is the dream and when we die, we wake up?"

Eye don't know why but Eye think about this all the time. It's like we enter another world or dimension when we are asleep. Sometimes our dreams are so peaceful and we tend to see people and places that we never seen before. Then we forget....how astonishing. This is far from our innerstanding. Physical death seems to be a mystery.

Now lets clear this up. Eye am proud of who Eye am and Eye love those who are apart of my culture and race. Eye am not ashamed or nor am Eye uncomfortable or afraid to embrace my culture in front of other races of people. That don't mean that Eye don't like other races or cultures of people. How can any person love or accept anyone else when they do not love and accept who they are or their own culture. Everyone should embrace their own heritage and culture. We are all human but we are all different for a reason and that's what makes the world so beautiful. So when Eye uplift Black people or embrace my culture, don't take it as me being prejudice towards other races. There is good and evil in every race of people so Eye always judge a person off their actions rather than how their outer appearance looks.

BLACK POWER IS NEITHER RACIST NOR IS IT THE HATRED OF OTHERS. IT IS A SPIRITUAL WAY OF LIFE PROMOTING SELF LOVE, DETERMINATION AND THE WELL-BEING OF OUR PEOPLE. WE MUST NEVER ALLOW ANYONE TO DISCOURAGE THIS

People who are "Spiritually Minded" tend to suffer from anxiety and depression more. But this is because their eyes are open to a world that is in need of repair. They literally have an increased ability to feel the emotions of people around them. This can be a gift and a curse. It really doesn't causes me depression but my mind never turns off and sometimes Eye can be mentally drained.

"Of what purpose is it to build walls that block the light and then strive for enlightenment?"

"A problem resolved in your heart is often no longer an issue for your mind,"

"Once you control their minds, you control their emotions, after you control their emotions, you control their bodies...after you control their bodies, you control their faith, once you control their faith, you control their soul with fear of losing it.."

Love Relationships have become a deadly place to be in some people's lives. Their relations become a prison or court room. Too much insecurity, envy, and control. So Eye came up with this logic.....Listen closely...Eye am about to give you the game. Those who are in relationships or whatever the case may be...If you are the one who is insecure or always worried about someone cheating on you, you need to stop. Jealous & envy is a dangerous thing and also bad for your health. If that person is with you, their with you...just do what you suppose to be doing. You see, a lot of you are not doing what your suppose to be doing and that's why you get so insecure when your partner's attention goes somewhere else. But peep this, a person is going to cheat regardless if you nag & spy on that person or not. It's nothing you can do about it. You just have to know who you are with and hopefully their the right one. Have confidence in yourself and your relationship because all that worrying and stressing about other people trying to steal your partner is not important. People are going always admire and find the person you with attractive no matter where you go. It's totally different when someone is disrespecting you purposely trying to steal what you have. But don't be so much worried about who want the person that you are with, just take care of your business. Your relationships will be so much less stressful. Trust me, insecurities & jealousy destroys relationships and pushes your partner away mentally & physically. That fire the both of you have will burn out & your relationship will become like a prison, dull & boring.
*How can a person make someone be faithful when they don't want to?? That's not realistic. You will stress yourself into having a nervous breakdown or having a heart-attack trying to do that. Stress causes you to age quickly.

    You know what, Eye really get tired of seeing fatherless kids running around especially little boys and teens.

    Men...where we're you when your Sun(son) was in the womb for 9months? Where were you when your Sun entered this world crying? Where were you when the Woman needed you to help her raise this boy into a Man?. Where were you when your

Sun was wondering why you didn't love him? Where were you when your Sun cried himself to sleep wishing he had a father to bond with? Where were you when your Sun was having sex and getting these girls pregnant, not knowing how to love a woman? Where were you when your Sun decided to try drugs, just to fit in and heal the pain inside? Where were you when your Sun decided to join a gang, just because he wanted to feel loved or wanted? Where were you when you knew that he was out of control and YOU DID NOTHING ABOUT IT??? WHERE WERE YOU WHEN YOUR SON WAS SCREAMING FOR YOU AS HE TOOK HIS LAST BREATH, WISHING THAT YOU COME AND SAVE HIM FROM DYING? Where were you?

*By Not being there, you have damaged our women. They do not trust or respect you anymore. She does not depend on you anymore. She does not feel secure or protected by you anymore, but she continues to love you while you only love yourself..

If A Man cannot be there for his children to love and protect them, what makes you think that he will be there to love and protect the woman?

Being there for your children is more than just being there. It's about spending that quality time. This should always come first, no matter what. Don't wait till later to make time, just to show up at the funeral, to see your child lying there, lifeless. Your too late.

The reason why some Men don't know how to love or treat a woman is because they never seen a real Man love their mother. And likewise to the Woman...the reason why she don't know how to love or treat a man is because she never seen a real woman love their father or any man.

Now Eye will take a moment to give you The Solution to some of our problems that we struggle within ourselves....

Remember as Eye told you before, this is no ordinary

book. Your average book will take its own turn and will have you trying to figure out and follow the direction it is going in. This novel is a conversation linked inside your soul to move your spirit while its walking with you in a physical form. It hugs and nurtures you as you think about the things that you are holding in, and while your feeling that no one will truly understand what you are going through. I will walk with you through the darkest tunnel and I will climb with you to the highest mountain. Different situations and problems can have all sorts of different solutions. So no one should be capable of giving you the text book love of what they have been programmed to say to you, because we are all created the same but with different spirits & different standards, linked to one common ground. Sometimes the only person we can really trust, is ourselves. We have to seek to be brilliant individuals, but before the beginning of brilliance, there must be chaos. Before a brilliant person begins something great, they must look foolish to the crowd. Also don't be deceived by your beliefs, because it does not make you a better person, your actions do. We cannot walk unless we learn to crawl, and we cannot crawl unless we are place on the ground to be willing to move on our own. No matter how much we deny it, most of us need love, support, guidance, and someone who will really touch that empty feeling of insecurity inside of us. Emotions from our unstable heart must be pushed to the side in order for the mind to be willing to open. Everything starts in the mind and once the mind is right within, then it will lead to positive, productive actions. So do you choose to be apart of the Problem or the Solution?

"Sometimes you have to love and care for someone so much that it hurts the pain inside of them."

PHASE 1

"Loving & Embracing your True self, & Overcoming the Obstacles of Insecurity, Anger, & Self-Hatred"

Getting To Know Yourself

When the storm comes, its seems like you are the only one getting afflicted by the wind. The rain comes down so hard that you need more than just an umbrella because your still getting rain on. They tell you to just love yourself, pray, and everything will be just fine. But how do you love yourself when you don't even know who you are. All your life you have been pretending to be something that's fitting & pleasing to the crowd, and so much love was given away, that there was none left for yourself.

"Please take me away from this strange place and fulfill this empty feeling inside of me." This is what is said in most individuals minds on a day to day basis. I was too, a victim of this storm. No knowledge of self, no purpose, or no directions to any destinations. Sometimes we have to just to shut the door on the world, focus, and get to know ourselves a little better. What do we really like to do before we are influenced by the crowd to act out of character? What do we love about ourselves and what do we
need to work on? What makes us laugh, cry, smile or frown? Spending time with ourselves can be quite peaceful & relaxing to our soul. If we can't learn to get along with ourselves, how can we really get along with others? We will do nothing but go along with others, there's a huge difference. Seeking within yourself by writing down what you feel inside will cause you to achieve a true connection within yourself. We all can put makeup on, dress up

the outside, and put on an act, but no matter what, we cannot ignore whats going on in the inside. We will always feel that same pain until we decide to remove that thorn in our side that keeps nagging us. Never stay in the position where you are holding your emotions in and hiding how you really feel about things. By doing this, you are only loosing yourself and your true identity. If you have to talk to yourself sometimes just to vent what you feel, do so. A cluttered mind & heart forms an unstable personality. Take yourself out on dates, out to eat, walks in the park, or even spend a little time alone at the beach. Become one with yourself.

"Why did the Creator make me this way?, you might asked. Everyone has their own purpose, their own talents, their own special gifts. So never try to compare yourself to anyone because you will either idolize them too much or you will envy them. Then you will look back at yourself and start to doubt your own abilities. You must move at your own pace, while never trying to keep up with the world. Never find yourself, being in a rush to go nowhere.

Pay attention to the vibes you get from people or the certain energies you receive within yourself. You don't want to be in a crowd of individuals wondering "why am I here?" Not knowing yourself will cause you to try to find yourself in others. You will just experience whatever the majority of the popular people are doing. Have control of yourself because if you fail to do so, someone will always have control of you and your mind. You might seem to get angry with others and irritated at times because of your lack of security. Keep pushing yourself to be more than you designed yourself to be. Then you will just sit back and realize that you are an awesome, original individual.

Acknowledging The Inner & Outer Beauty

You have to realize that you hold your own standard of beauty. Never let the media or the crowd convince or deceive you to think that true beauty is only one certain way to look. The most amazing thing about being beautiful is that there are many different styles & ways of being beautiful. Everything must start within. Whatever is going on in the inside will be reflected on the outside. Just like a gift that is wrapped so beautifully on the outside but when you open it up, there is nothing inside. Most of the time we dress up the outside to hide whats really going on in the inside, but eventually we will see right through the decorations.

  First we have to accept the way that we were created & embrace every feature about ourselves. You don't have to search for it because it is already there whenever you look in the mirror. While repeatedly say this to yourself, "Eye Am Beautiful and Eye believe in myself", you will receive and feel the positive energies & vibrations that you need to finally accept your natural beauty. Truly love yourself and you will draw love to you. Respect yourself and you will draw respect back. Sometimes other people will treat you how they perceive you to be.

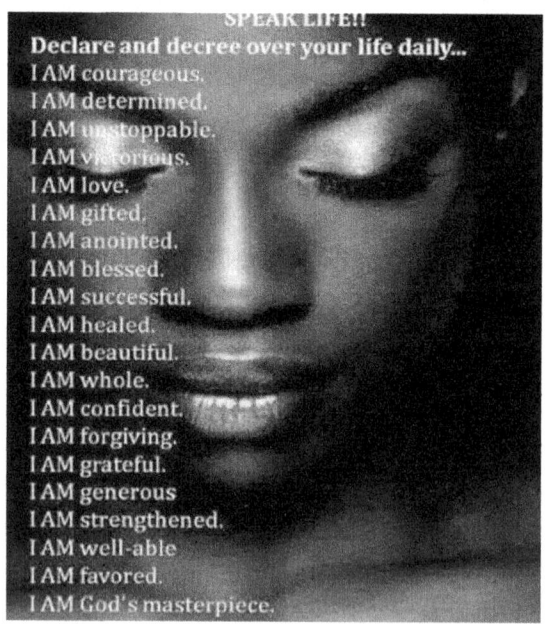

SPEAK LIFE!!
Declare and decree over your life daily...
I AM courageous.
I AM determined.
I AM unstoppable.
I AM victorious.
I AM love.
I AM gifted.
I AM anointed.
I AM blessed.
I AM successful.
I AM healed.
I AM beautiful.
I AM whole.
I AM confident.
I AM forgiving.
I AM grateful.
I AM generous.
I AM strengthened.
I AM well-able
I AM favored.
I AM God's masterpiece.

Men must first understand this phrase when they are mainly focus on the outer appearances of a woman, while they do not take the time to focus on the beauty within a woman....

"Too much Candy will spoil your appetite before a full course meal...Too much fast food will corrupt the mind while a healthy home cook meal will nurture the mind & body....So, just like the old school parents use to say...."finish your food before you eat that candy."

"Women, if you are only focus on your looks, it will get you no further than the bedroom."

*in other words...make sure that person feeds your soul first before she trick or treat you with her candy....

If your physical appearances is not effecting your health....please love & embrace yourself....and if you want or desire to look a certain way....do it because YOU WANT TO, not because someone is forcing you to or convincing you that you are not beautiful enough. Remember you are whatever you "Think" of yourself.

Conquer these seven steps & you will acknowledge your beauty within.

1. Self-Awareness
2. Self-Exploration
3. Self-Discovery
4. Self-Understanding
5. Self-Love
6. Self-transformation
7. Self-Mastery

Your beauty must start within. Your character plays a huge role that will have an effect on your outer appearances. People will absorb the energy that you put out and they will feel the positive or negative vibrations that you are giving off. Those vibrations can be a vision of beauty or a vision that's not so worth admiring. Don't protect your outer beauty when your insides is dying and is so unattractive . Be the individual who is in the process of learning to know, accept, and love yourself on all levels, Mind, Body, & Spirit. Be the individual who focus on personal growth and self awareness, experiences a life, increasingly filled with peace, love, joy, passion and fun. You should understand that you have unlimited capacity to make your life be anything you want. Be an inspiration to those around you and have that sense of gratitude & abundance. After this, you will be beautiful within and without.

Overcoming Insecurities

Sometimes you will have that feeling when you are just tired & things may seem as they will never change because you are experiencing the same routine everyday. Sometimes you may feel insecure about yourself or feel down at times. All this is normal, so never think to yourself that you are loosing it. Whatever doubts, insecurities, or pain that's holding you down, you must take time out to release it. Release all negative energies. Enter in a quiet place or room to take deep breaths while exhaling. Think about all the great things & abilities that you are blessed with. Imagine the places you desire to see and visit. Visualize how you want to see your future and keep that picture in your mind at all times as motivation for you as you walk through your journey in life. Always except and embrace your own standard of beauty and never try to compete or compare yourself to anyone. Your creator made you exactly the way you was suppose to be because we were all made differently and that's the beauty of it.

Take your power back from those who hurt you because you have so much love to give and to receive. Never let anyone put road blocks in your life but rather cleanse your soul and renew your mind. Free yourself of those chains and be FREE!! LIVE!!!

because you have so much life to live. LIVE!! Enjoy and embrace every second of your life. Stay smiling, it looks good on you.

  Eye personally have become like Poetry in a world that's still trying to learn the alphabet. So don't worry if others don't seem to understand you at the moment, because our minds are all quite different. Hold on to your own self-will and never give it up to someone's opinion because a part of you will die every time. Know the world within yourself, and never look for yourself in the world. For this would be to project your illusion. You will always find yourself being compared to a world that you can't keep up with, and then you will feel that insecurity blanket of doubt in yourself. When you overcome the media, television, music and entertainment, then you will overcome the insecurities within those illusions that you have created for yourself.

  The hardest battle you will ever fight, is the battle within yourself. Most people cannot see their true self because they have pulled the world over their eyes. Insecurities can be your prison if you don't obtain the confidence to break free. What is stopping you from being you? Have you lost yourself? Who are you? Maybe you need to sit and talk with someone who cares for you, or who can help open your mind. Tell them how you feel and stop pretending. Just to be curious, ask other how they feel and think of you.

  One day you will realize that you are the only one holding yourself in chains. Break free because only you hold the key of life. Guess what? The person that you see in the mirror that is looking back at you, knows that you are beautiful and believes in you. When you truly love and believe in yourself, you will attract others who truly love and believe in you as well.

  Hey!, Beautiful Woman...."Never, ever feel like you are nothing or that you are not appreciated. Never feel that you are hopeless & things will never get any better, regardless of any situation. Never look down or loose confidence in yourself over a foolish individual."

"Real Men need you & We love & admire everything about you. Just hold your head.....there is a smoother road ahead of you, right after you finish walking down that rocky road. We all go through hell, & your never alone. Just make sure you keep that smile when Heaven is at your door."

"The people who hurt you, only bent you because you was too powerful to be broken.....Your still standing right? So continue walking that beautiful walk & never look back unless your pulling a love one beside you, to walk together in unity. Cry it out if you have to....it cleanses the soul."

Eye told this woman one day that she was very beautiful and she didn't believe me. In return, she responded to me and said that her hair wasn't done and she didn't have any makeup on. Then Eye said, "Exactly, You don't have to try so hard, you are already beautiful....So why cover up perfection?"

A beautiful woman entered a relationship with a Man who she loved and desired so much for a long time. She was willing to change anything that he didn't approve of or like about her character. Also she was willing to alter her physical appearances. So what do you think happened when that Man got tired of her and left? Yes! Exactly...she lost herself and made it up in her mind that she was nothing. She didn't consider herself beautiful anymore. She wondered how could a man leave her when she have changed everything for him. She suffered from a one-sided relationship.

Some might say, "How can a Man become insecure?" Trust me, it happens. When a Man sets his goals or dreams that he has for himself real high and he doesn't reach it in the time that he predicted, he gets down on himself. This is why you never put time or age on things. It will happen when it will happen. Just continue to do your part. Hard work and dedication always pays off even when your in doubt sometimes. Never stop when you are tired.....Stop when you are finish.

Observing and watching everyone succeed will only make it worst for you. Their time and your time is totally different. So never compare yourself or try to compete with anyone. A certain title or accomplishment does not determine your manhood.

Physical appearance should never determine who you really are. If you are uncomfortable with your body, do something about it.....motivate yourself. Stop looking at others wishing and fantasizing....become one with your goal or whatever you strive to be.

In order to get to your true self & overcome your insecurities, you must be reborn within. You must remove all illusions from your mind on how you should look. Even if you have to start all over with your appearance. You may have to find your true self underneath the cover up. This will be the hardest thing for you to do, but at the end of the day it will be worth it. Break free from mental slavery & build back what you have destroyed.

"CONTROL TIME"

Eye turned my back on the world while facing the world, just to get away from the world.

Becoming One with self & everything around me.

The things that you worry about is non-existence to me.

How can you see when the mind is blind. You move when the world tells you to move.

But Me, Eye Control Time!!

Dealing with Anger & Removing Self-hatred

In our lives, we all get a little angry at times. Some of us will even act violently on it....but that is something that has to be kept under control. Believe it or not but a lot of anger can lead to self-hatred. It makes us ugly on the inside as well as on the outside.

"When there is no enemy within, the enemy outside, can do no harm."

If you realized how powerful your thoughts are, you would never think a negative thought. So be careful what you fill and allow to come in your mind. Your thoughts eventually become you.....so if it's mostly negativity, then you will become an unstable, emotional thinker, struggling to keep a balance. Negativity wouldn't be so popular if we didn't support it.

"When the world seems so loud, and is moving so rapidly.....who will take the timeout, just to hear you scream??"

"THE LAW OF ATTRACTION"

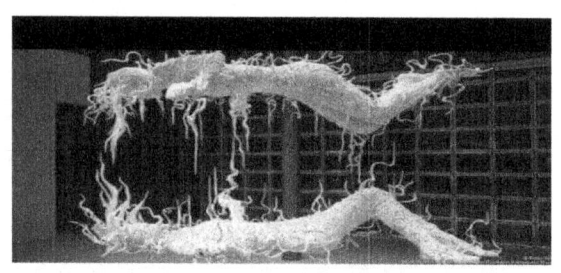

You attract into your life a reflection of what you think. But you also attract into your life what you judge. If you think people are dishonest, you attract dishonest people. If you are focused on a sickness or disease, you attract more. If you focus on poverty or lack, you gain nothing more than an empty bank account. Everything you hold in your conscious thought becomes your cage and your reality. See abundance, see honesty in all, embrace good, emotionally healthy people.

If you really think about it and pay attention. People who are spiritually minded tend to suffer from anxiety and depression more. This is because their eyes are open to a world that is in need of repair. They literally have an increased ability to feel the emotions of people around them.

Concerning myself, Eye tend to not get depressed at all but my mind never turns off. Eye always feel others emotions before they even speak. It can be good, weird, uncomfortable, and scary sometimes.

Changes: Is what many of us hate doing, but if you are tired of the same routine in your life, then maybe its time to change and graduate from that. Maybe it's your job or a bad relationship that you feel isn't going anywhere. When we put ourselves in certain situations in life, we learn from these things either good or bad. After that, we keep building on it if necessary, or we decide to let it go if we see no process of growth.

A lot of us are afraid of change because we have gotten too comfortable of where we are we are in life at the moment. We wake up everyday punishing ourselves with the same routine that we hate doing. It's like we have no desire to graduate and move on to the next level. We must convince ourselves that there is always something greater. We have too much living to do and no matter what our age is, we have to make responsible changes and not be afraid of taking risks. Be more, do more and give each day your all. Graduate from where you are and keep elevating in life physically, mentally, and spiritually.

Don't fall so much in love with your surroundings that you end up having no drive to seek outside your box. That moment when you become comfortable, is the moment that you stop living. There is a big difference from just being alive and actually living.

"Beware of destination addiction: The idea that happiness is in the next place, the next job, or even with the next partner. Until you give up the idea that happiness is somewhere else, it will never be where you are."

You know....sometimes it is very hard to talk to certain individuals because they are so cautious that they walk around with their guards up all the time. Eye never let negative people that Eye run across in my life, force me to build walls and to have my guards up all the time. These people do not deserve that kind of power over me to change my true character. When people walk around with their guards up all the time, it will be very hard for them to see the light in those that they may run across. If those walls that you built are too high, hoe can you really see a person for who they truly is?

"Of what purpose is it to build walls that block the light and then strive for enlightenment?"

This is a quote that sat well with me in my spirit, from Robert Green's book "The 48 Laws of Power".....

"If you enter an action with less than total confidence, you set up obstacles in your own path."
-Robert Green

Most of the time, Eye can care less about who Eye piss off or make angry when Eye am just being me. They may not like everything that Eye say but deep down inside they know that there is some logical truth in my words.

Truth and emotions don't mix well at all. You must have a strong mind to face the reality of things. A weak mind will get your feelings hurt every time and it will always leave you emotional. So Eye say that to say this.....They're either using you, helping you, or watching you.

"The more Eye learn the more Eye know the more Eye realize that Eye don't know what Eye thought Eye knew- Only to find out that what Eye now know Eye wish Eye didn't know at all!

Now who's really afraid to face what they see in the mirror? Eye will give you a simple technique and method to overcome any kind of denial or finding it hard by admitting that you have a problem that you are really embarrassed about. Thinking and praying about it all the time is not going to make it magically disappear.

Maybe you have a physical health problem that you are afraid to check out. Maybe you are addicted to gambling or shopping and you feel that it is getting out of hand. Maybe you feel that you are overweight, too skinny, or not beautiful enough and you feel rather ugly at times. Maybe you have a sex addition or lust problem. What is more important is that you faced them.

Get in front of a large mirror. Stare at your reflection. Speak aloud by telling yourself three things that you like about yourself. Accept the person that's looking back at you. Tell yourself that you are struggling and that you admit that this is the problem that has been bringing you down.

Out loud in a clear voice, tell yourself about the problems that you have been avoiding. Repeat your statement multiple times until you get comfortable with it. Now commit to taking a step to resolve this problem or problems within the next 24 hours. Say to yourself what you are planning to do until you are sure of it.

After you have accomplished this method, congratulate yourself for your courage and honesty. Smile and release that negative energy and extra weight off your shoulders.

"If you suffer, it is because of you. If you feel blissful, it is because of you. Nobody else is responsible- only you alone. You are your hell and your heaven too."
-OSHO

Some beautiful people are born to repair and heal the mind, heart and soul of others. That's why should appreciate every positive and caring person that we encounter. We should be willing to just listen rather than so quick to be offended and make excuses.

"Through WISDOM a house is built and by understanding it is established by KNOWLEDGE, the rooms are filled with all precious and pleasant riches."

"Be someone who makes someone else look forward to tomorrow."

"If you wish to create a new reality, you must first let go of the one that no longer serves you. A glass that is already full, cannot hold more water. It must be emptied first"

-Peace is so important to have within yourself-

Positive
Energy
Activates
Constant
Elevation

    Chess is one of the most greatest games ever invented. Eye love chess because life is chess. Everything in life is about strategies, sacrifices, protection, and promotion (self elevation). You may loose people (pawns)....you may even so-call loose the game, but it will take a whole lot of thinking, strategies, and fighting to do so. At the end of the day, you cannot really loose a chess game(life). The only way you can really loose in chess(Life), is if you don't give it your all and not learn from your mistakes. One false move and you will loose your freedom and become conquered mentally and physically. Then you have to line the chess pieces back up and try again. In other words, you have to pick yourself up when you fall, and keep fighting. Next time, come with a different approach or strategy.

    F.Y.I. There would be no game of chess if the pawns refused to play. Don't feed the beast because you will only make the enemy stronger with your emotions, frustrations, negativity, promotion, & weak counter attacks. If you want to check him....his kingdom must stay divided & fall within itself. His Queen, Bishop, Knight, & Rook has to betray him to leave him standing alone to fall. Once the pawns wise up and become their own leaders and be promoted, they gain power and confidence to not be moved or provoked against their own will.

    "Eye sit back and observe EVERY person in my life. Eye know who supports me, down for me who keeps it 100. Eye don't say anything, but Eye know."

"You can't let praise or criticism get to you. It's a weakness to get caught up in either one."

"Life is given, Death is a choice."

THE COST OF AMBITION

*Late nights, early mornings.
*Lots of associates, very few friends.
*You will be single unless you're lucky enough to find someone who innerstands your lifestyle.
*People will want you to do good, but never better than them.
For these reasons, you will do many things alone.

    Never let anyone stop or slow you down from accomplishing the goals you set out in your life. If you want something, you work hard for it and grab it. If you decide to be an athlete and you desire to play professional sports....you need to give a 100% work ethic when you are training. If you are not determined to be the best athlete when you step foot on the field or court when the game starts, you might as well stay on the bench and not play. Don;t even waste your time or your teammates time, including the ones thst are supporting you. It's going to get real hard, maybe very exhausting at times, but you have to embrace that pain and keep fighting. Never let ANYONE see you fatigue or hurting. Stick your chess out and say, "What else do you got for me?" Always absorb positive energy and support from those around you. Stay motivated and if there is no one around you to keep you motivated, learn to motivate yourself.

    Be Perfect. Being perfect is being honest and real with yourself while knowing that you are giving your all into what you are doing. It's about not letting yourself and other down around you. Being the best is knowing for sure that you did the absolute best that you can. Always have fun, that's important as well. You only loose when you quit or give up. Use this concept of The Cost of Ambition with any and everything that you decide to do in life.

You know, when all this negativity and evil that's going on in the world, Eye am no longer interested in it. Meaning that Eye will not put any energy into it and worry about what others are doing. Eye am only concerned about the path that Eye choose to take as Eye manifest my own destiny. Eye will not absorb those negative energies from individuals around me but only unify with those individuals who are willing to elevate with me or inspire and motivate me to grow. The world doesn't create me, Eye create my own world. Eye will not feed the beast.

"One day, you'll be a memory for some people. Do your best, to be a good one."

"Every minute you are angry, you loose sixty seconds of your happiness"

-Stress kills and many of us are dying slowly by the minute from the inside out.-

"Be patient with everyone, but above all with yourself. Do not be disheartened by your imperfections, but always rise up with fresh courage."

These are the 5 most important people to have on your team. They are known as the Fab 5.
1. The one who Encourages
2. The Dreamer
3. The Truth Teller
4. The Action Taker
5. The Believer

And guess what, they can all be the same person.....YOU!

"In this life people will continue to use you for their own benefit but will never care for you the way you care for them. This is one of the hardest emotional things to deal with. As time pass, you start to heal and blessings seem to come out of nowhere in your favor. So if you know your heart was in the right place the whole time....don't worry, troubles won't last long and those sunny days will never turn back to rain."

"you break yourself just to fix somebody else"

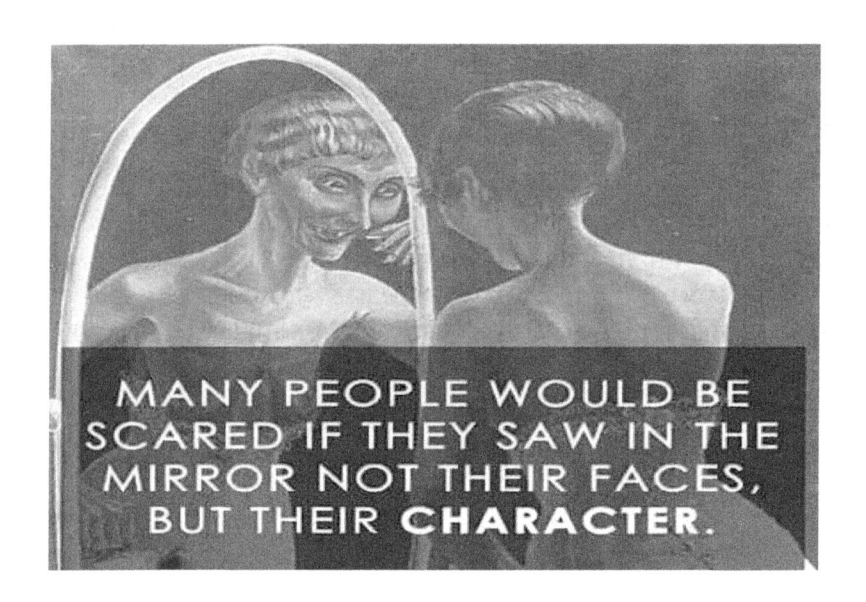

> MANY PEOPLE WOULD BE SCARED IF THEY SAW IN THE MIRROR NOT THEIR FACES, BUT THEIR **CHARACTER**.

"You can't keep trying to empower & uplift certain people if they have no intentions of doing right and bettering themselves. All you doing is making them comfortable and giving them band-aids when they really need stitches. If a person don't see any wrong and how they are living, then they will not change."

Stop pampering people's ignorance and give them strict discipline on the things they need to hear. Hurt their feelings with the TRUTH rather than trying to make them feel good with a LIE. If not, you are helping them destroy themselves. All this King & Queen talk has no effect if you are not living like one.

As a Real, Alpha Man, Eye will say this to the Black Woman since other so-called conscious men are afraid to tell their women this....maybe their trying to gain points or make them like them more, but me, Eye am gonna give u REAL. ALL BLACK WOMEN OR ANY OTHER RACE OF WOMEN ARE NOT QUEENS OR GODDESSES, don't get it twisted. Just because you have melanin don't make you are Royalty. You have to earn that title and live up to it. By the way it is not a title but rather a way of life. Majority of our Women are broken and until they admit that, our nation will never be at its full strength. We will remain weak until our Women wake up and start moving mountains. Fix your attitudes, get rid of all that bitterness, anger, hate, insecurity, competitive thinking, etc,etc. Stop having babies by these sorry Men, just because you want someone to Love you unconditionally. Stop arguing and fighting with Men....hold on to your feminine ways as well as your strength. Stop trying to do what Men do, you are made to do greater things on a whole another level.

     Your outer beauty means nothing if your inner-self is so ugly and unattractive. From all those self-pictures and body shots you take and post on social media....If that's all you have to offer, then Eye am not impressed. You are only attracting and drawing in shallow, weak, emasculated, thirsty Men who only see you as an image that he lust for. These men do not really care about you. Don't let those Likes pump your head up...it means nothing!!

     Eye Love my Women too much to lie to them. So tired of seeing them not at their full potential. Black Women...no matter how you present yourself and what image you try to portray. Eye see straight through your mask, right into your soul, while knowing that you never encountered a King that made you tremble with Love & Compassion.

-EYE DON'T THROW SHADE, EYE SHADE LIGHT-

FORGIVENESS

This image is the most powerful art piece this year. The sculpture of 2 adults after a disagreement sitting with their back to each other. Yet, the inner child in both of them simply wants to connect. Age has taught us much, but what we can't live without is ego, hatred and grudges that prevent us from forgiving and moving ahead. The free spirit exhibited by children is our true nature.

We must really innerstand what FORGIVENESS really means. You cannot keep walking around with this hate for one another or other kinds of people regardless of what they have done. Forgiveness does not mean that you accept them & continue to let them keep running over you. Forgiveness means that you take back your power emotionally and mentally so you would be able to move on in a productive way.

Unbalanced and negative emotions will have you at a stand still in life of always complaining, pointing the finger and playing the victim. For an example, some Pro Black people hate white people and some white people hate black people, and they made it up in their mind that they will never forgive. They have lost their power and made their enemy feel so good knowing that they still have power over their emotions. This only stops them from accomplishing things that really matter and actually it is actually stopping them from growth of themselves and their people. When you forgive people, you will not allow the same mistakes to happen again. You forgive them enough to correct them or take action to balance the scale.

Honestly it's really not in us to hate anyone when we are fully conscious and have reached our Crown Chakra. We can rebuke, divide or even protect ourselves without coming to a point where we actually hate an individual. Most people are just hurt and confused, so they hide their true feeling with a hate mask. All their doing in bringing in more negative energies and vibrations to themselves and it will effect them mentally, physically, spiritually, and emotionally. These people are easy to control.

There are scriptures in the Bible & Qur'an where it says to make yourself like a child with a pure, innocent heart and clear mind, and you will see the kingdom of heaven...Now Eye innerstand the Logic of those scriptures. No matter what you do to a child, that child will continue to Love and Forgive you. A lot of people want their Higher Power whom they never seen to forgive them of their short comings, but they have no desire to forgive the people of their short coming that they see everyday."

HAPPINESS IS.....

TURNING YOUR HOBBY INTO A PAID JOB

Eye can truly say that Eye am very happy and have peace within and without. This is not to knock anyone who works for other people...everyone has their own lives.

Concerning myself, Eye just couldn't work for anyone and keep sitting back watching these Bosses get rich off my labor when Eye can be doing what their doing. Eye stopped doubting myself and proved to myself of how great Eye am. Meditated and prayed about it and recognized the abilities that the Most High blesses me with. Eye had to align all the energies and vibrations in the Universe to set up my path.

Well, Eye am rich in spirit but concerning money, Not yet. Eye just know how to balance out things to make it comfortably for my family. Eye do not buy things Eye can't afford or try to live above my means. Eye do not do car payments, if Eye can't afford to buy it cash, then Eye don't need it. Eye innerstand the economic games out there and how much money we loose by leasing cars.

Eye noticed that most people are not happy working for other people. They force themselves to be happy. There never at home and they slave themselves just to pay bills. They slave themselves just to stunt and show off in a car that they can't afford. This is where the attitudes in most people come from for no reason. If you have talents or goals, why give up on them just to get hired by someone else to achieve their goals? Honestly, there is no such thing as a struggle. Many people have convinced themselves that there is a struggle because they depend on their Oppressor to take care of them and finance them.

      Make it to where your significant other do not have to stress themselves at a job. Let their job be just a place just to get out the house just to make extra money, and likewise to us that have Boss/Ownership/Freedom goals...make it to a point where u are using these jobs to invest in your own.

      Eye worry about nothing. Eye help those in need when Eye have nothing because Eye know the power of the Universe and the Law of Attraction. Sometimes you have it, sometimes you don't. We make it harder on ourselves because of our selfishness and envy towards one another. All we do is compete with each other. That's why some of us walk around so angry with stank attitudes.

      If you choose to spend your life being a worker, that's fine, nothing wrong with that....but concerning me, Eye only get excited as being my own Boss and controlling my own time. If you have dreams, wake up and turn them into a Reality. The more Eye elevate the more Eye become so conscious to never settle for a check just to get by. That's not living to me, that's gasping for air while begging for your life. It changes your true character and you will eventually loose yourself by acting a certain way just to keep your job. Everything that you spend a lot of time on you should get paid for it. Eye truly believe that or you are just wasting valuable time.

The Heart of A Man

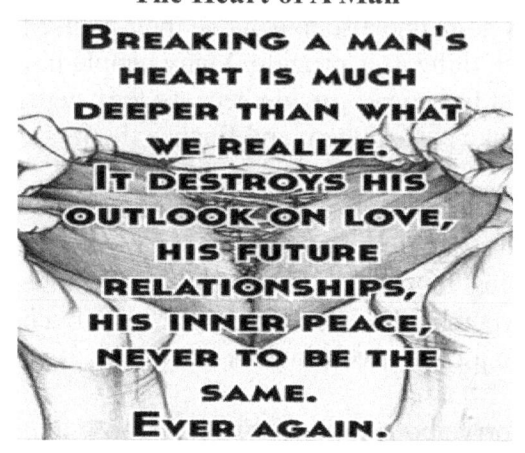

> **BREAKING A MAN'S HEART IS MUCH DEEPER THAN WHAT WE REALIZE. IT DESTROYS HIS OUTLOOK ON LOVE, HIS FUTURE RELATIONSHIPS, HIS INNER PEACE, NEVER TO BE THE SAME. EVER AGAIN.**

What if Eye told you that every man desires to be held as tight as a woman, but his pride will never allow him to admit to it. A woman really controls a man's character. She has the influence to mold him or break him. Eye see a lot of broken Men who have gotten their hearts broken by that one woman who have turned them so cold where they are too afraid to get close to a real strong woman again. He's so afraid where he only will mess around with insecure women who will give him cheap pleasures that will only satisfy his lust within himself. He needs many insecure women in his life to keep him from feeling lonely at times, but at the end of the day, he wants to really love and be loved by that one woman, but he has no courage to do so. He's afraid of what will happen to him mentally If he gives his heart to another. So he only hangs around other insecure Men who are also afraid of uniting with a strong woman who loves strong. Also these Men get together and prey on the weak and insecure women and if he does decide to unite with a strong woman, he will keep those insecure women on the side just just as a back up plan if he gets his heart broken again. Not knowing that this is his downfall...He fears that Woman's love so much because he cannot bear the pain anymore from another broken heart.

Men will try to fool you into thinking that they have no heart or feelings. Most of them have been broken by strong women who took control of their hearts. Most Men are Beta Males and very few are Alpha Males. Alpha Males rises to the occasion and molds the woman and takes control in Unity.

"Some people aren't loyal to you. They are loyal to their need of you. Once their needs change, so does their loyalty."

You know, sometimes if you try to encourage a negative person to do better and to be a better person, they will get mad at you, hate you, or even talk behind your back and say that you are judging them.

But if you agree with a negative person and blame others for everything like they do.....watch how they unite with you and love you. Also they will pretend to be down with you as long as you play the victim with them and continue to point fingers at everyone else but themselves. Just because these negative people have no dive or goals in life to accomplish, they don't want you to have none either. They will convince you that the world is on its verge to end and that we are all doomed, so why even bother to enjoy your life and be something. Stay away from these people who get thrills off negative energy in this world. Their demons are very contagious. Smile sometimes, It looks so good on you.

Follow The Pyramid

YES, EYE DID IT!

EYE WILL DO IT.

EYE CAN DO IT.

EYE WILL TRY TO DO IT.

HOW DO EYE DO IT.

EYE WANT TO DO IT.

EYE CAN'T DO IT.

EYE WANT TO DO IT.

    The choice is yours. Don't let your current situation discourage you. Everyday is a stepping stone in your life. How can you see how far you can go if you don't take the first step? Nothing is too hard for you. If someone else can do it, why not you?

"Just because my path is different, it doesn't mean Eye am lost."

    Sometimes people get so sure of their beliefs that it makes them so arrogant where it turns into hate for others who believe differently, while they continue to loose their morals at the same time. Sometimes people tend to suffer a lot, feel depressed often, or keep going through the same struggles. All the time it is not a test from GOD. The reality is that they are not living the way they suppose to live....meaning, their foul and they know it. People must take full responsibility for their actions.

    Someday everyone must elevate their mind mentally and spiritually, and realize that their beliefs have no power unless their actions are reflecting off of what they believe in. There is some truth in every belief system and there are many ways to connect with the Higher Power and the God within you. Eye am sorry that you were convinced by men of power to think that there is only one way. Don't you find it awkward that we all go through the same struggles and receive some of the same blessings sometimes, regardless of what we believe in or worship? The objective is to learn from those struggles and how to avoid them from keep happening all over again. Now that's the God in you.

      People must stop judging people off of what they believe in but rather see the fruit that person bear and how they live. Then they will see who they really are behind that religious or conscious mask that they wear. Love, Hate, and Envy cannot exist in a righteous person all at the same time. If so, that person is unbalanced and not right within, regardless of what they believe. They are either on the side of good or on the side of evil. There is a spiritual war going on filled with Gods, Devils, Angels, and Demons.

> "If the church does not recapture it's prophetic zeal, it will become an irrelevant social club without moral or spiritual authority."
>
> *-Martin Luther King Jr.*

      In reference to M.L.K.'s quote, Eye have a story to tell that happened recently. Eye was driving around and Eye got a little thirsty, so Eye decided stopped at a Exxon Mobile Station to get a cold drink. As Eye was at the counter, ready to check out, this elderly Man came up behind me and ask me what church Eye attended. So Eye politely told him that Eye was the church. He smiled. So Eye corrected him and said, "Are you asking me what building Eye attend?" His face expression changed and he told me if Eye am not apart of a church to come to his. So Eye sat their and listened to him for about 15mins while he promote his business(church).

Honestly my mind wondered off while he was talking and Eye noticed a young Black Woman walking by with a stroller. After this Man finished talking Eye decided to leave. As Eye passed up the woman with the stroller, Eye realized that it was a little baby inside, so Eye kept driving. Then Eye started to analyze the situation. Eye was driving down this long street and it was nothing around but grass and trees, and the next neighborhood or store was almost 2miles away.

So Eye kept driving for awhile, then Eye stopped. Eye asked myself, "Where in the hell is she going and why is she walking in 100 degree heat with that baby?" Eye made a u-turn and decided to go back to see if she was still walking and she was.

Eye pulled up beside her with my hazard lights on, raised my window down and politely greeted myself. Eye told her Eye didn't want nothing from her, but was curious of why she was walking down this long street with her baby. She looked at me with a weird look and said that she has no choice and that she needed to get to Walgreens for her baby. Eye was like, "damn, that's a long walk...Eye can give you a ride because Eye am going that way."

She paused, stared at me with another weird look, as the sweat dripped down her face. Her baby finally open her eyes, looked at me and smiled. Then the woman said, "Okay, Eye trust you...Eye see it in your eyes that you are not crazy" Eye told her, "no you don't trust me because you don't know me, but if Eye was going to kill you, Eye would've already done it, so get it and get that baby out this Sun."

So while we were driving, Eye was asking her about herself and questions about where the father of her child was. She told me that she didn't know. Eye was like, "as in knowing where he is at the moment or you don't know where's he's at period?" She said she doesn't know period, because he left before the baby was born and haven't heard from him.

Too make a long story short, this really pissed me off, she is 22yrs old, stayed by herself, was engaged, and basically was used by a man that claimed he loved her. But Eye can't see how any Man can leave his woman when she is bearing his child. Eye know it wasn't none of my business, but some kind of energy or spirit wouldn't let me pass her up and let them keep walking in the Sun, especially that baby who was only 6months old. Eye waited for her as she got what she needed out the store and took them back home. She offered me gas money but Eye rejected it and told her she do not owe me anything and that Eye was just looking out for my Black Women and someone has to. Also Eye told her to not let that Black Man who left her, changed her concept about Black Men.....some of us do care.

As Eye drove off, that old Man that stopped me in the gas station popped up in my mind. And Eye guarantee he saw her and her baby walking, and just passed them by, without any concerned. Eye remember telling him that Eye was the church and that Eye didn't need a building to connect with God or to do his work. God's work is needed in the streets, not the building. Maybe if more people came from out the church buildings and into the street, they would be able to help more people in need instead of giving them just smooth and fancy words. We don't need Religion but rather we need morals to help one another physically. Churches have become just a social club filled with people of no morals and no intentions to help no anyone.

Eye thought about that situation all last night about how some women are just left alone with kids and no fathers. It's not just the man fault, it's takes two, but Eye do give the woman credit for never leaving their children. Men should be ashamed of themselves that does that.

If you want to go to church, fine, but make sure you are being the church as well.

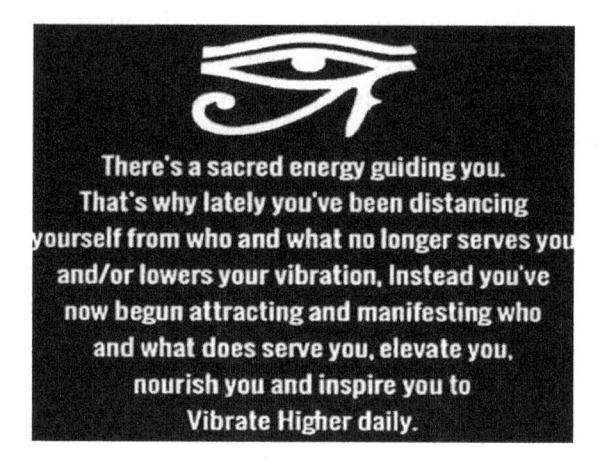

> There's a sacred energy guiding you. That's why lately you've been distancing yourself from who and what no longer serves you and/or lowers your vibration. Instead you've now begun attracting and manifesting who and what does serve you, elevate you, nourish you and inspire you to Vibrate Higher daily.

Eye know you may not take this seriously as Eye do, but never let anyone get comfortable calling you a "Nigga". Especially never let a white person, Asian, Mexican, etc,etc call you that. Eye don't care how cool y'all are. You may not believe this but the reality of that is when someone call you that, that means that they have no RESPECT for you. They may love you or may even ride for you from time to time, but they have no RESPECT for you. As long as you are on the same level as them or lower, they are cool with that...but as soon as you elevate from that ignorance, you become hated and they become intimidated by you. They start to making fun of your elevation. Eye don't even let Black people call me Nigga anymore...when they do, Eye do not respond to them.

Same thing goes for the word "b*tch", stop calling one another other that. We have to have some dignity for ourselves and know our self-worth.

> *"Is not about what they call you, but more about what you answer to."*
>
> *-African Proverb*

**Sometimes those
who don't socialize much
aren't actually anti-social,
they just have no tolerance
for drama and fake people.**

"Some of the best moments in life are the ones you can't tell anyone about."

    Many times, Eye was told that Eye live a secret life, but the reality is that some things you just want to keep to yourself and it's no ones business. You shouldn't need no ones approval or try to prove anything to anyone. So my advice to you is to not tell people all of your business. It will be less stressful for you, even for your family members. This doesn't mean you Love them any less.

> We worship Nature
>
> Don't laugh, we can prove it exists.

    Everything that you see all around you that grows and contains life is of God (The Most High, The Creator, The Universe). Everything that crawls, walks, flies, & makes all kinds of sounds is of The Most High. Even the dirt that you walk on daily, the wind that blows, the grass that grows, and the trees like those, is of the Most High. How can you say you Love God, whom you never seen and hate your different brothers and sisters that you see everyday, while not knowing that God is inside us all. When you hate your brothers and sisters and do wicked things to them, then you are only hating the God that you say you Love and Worship.

    Respect is even given to an enemy, but when you hate your enemy, then you have already lost the war. Having love for God's creation doesn't mean you accept and bow down to anything. Love is sometimes rebuking, protecting, and fighting for what is right even if you have to put an enemy out of their misery when they decides to let their hate take over them.

    Most wars are based off the Love of something....meaning the Love of money, Love of a certain land, Love of oil, Love of gold, diamonds, power, etc,etc...but that is the wrong kind of Love because it disrespects the law of nature and moralities of the World. So it's really a thin line between Love and Hate. Hate is when you destroy, tear down and kill without a conscious or reasonable cause. This earth was giving to us as a gift, for us to

Love and Respect the natures of this land. What Kind of fruit are you bearing on this land? That is the question and the reality that we are facing.

"Smooth Conscious words are easy to put together and powerful, conscious symbols, and clothes are easy to put on....but when it comes to actually living it, now that's the hard part. That's when you see who that actual person really is..."

"Stepping Stones....take things slow and really start within yourself and get your life in order. No one said it will be easy. It's very hard, but it comes naturally when you make it your life. Stop playing the conscious game and following the new trend before you get yourselves killed mentally, spiritually, and then physically."

"You cannot teach anyone anything productive if you are carrying hate in your heart, because you will eventually teach them to hate just like you."

Age only defines the frame of the body while the spirit and soul does not age, but only grows and feeds from knowledge and wisdom.

A book is just another item on a book shelf. Eye consider this words in motion, trapped in a cage, given a chance to break free into the minds of it's readers. Eye prefer my writings as not being in a book but rather as an exhale of energies being released in the form of literature, bleeding unto the canvas. The opened mind stops the bleeding and heals the opened wounds.

> Sometimes, opening your eyes may be the most painful thing you ever have to do.

"The most comfortable & dangerous mental state to be in is when you are purposely blinded to the Reality of things."

THE BEAT OF A WOMAN'S DRUM

"The Black Woman may not be perfect at times....She may can get a little emotional....She may turn cold or bitter at times...She may even become hard as a rock...and sometimes she may even loose herself to become something she is really not......but despite all that, The Black Woman will always be the first to Love and Support the Black Man in any situation if he deserves it or not. It's just in her nature to be God-like, no matter how much she tried to fight it. She cares too much. Don't be deceived when you think she has changed for the worst. She is only hurt and bent out of shape at the moment by us and the world, but we must stop her from breaking.

When the Black Woman walks, you will hear different beats of her drum, depending on that woman, it may be fast, it may be slow, or it may even skip a beat. Our mission is to keep her beats of her drum at a calm, steady pace. That way she will become secure, balanced, and emotionally stable."

*Make sure you pay attention to the beat of that Black Woman's drum.

The Fountain of Youth

You know, society is so programmed and messed up when majority of the people let their so-called age justify what they do. It's like they choose what you suppose to be doing at a particular age. Eye am not talking about dating, having or sex, or using drugs or alcohol. Eye am talking about the physical things you decide to do in your life for fun or choose to do in your spare time or make a career.

You have people that say, "Well you too young or old to be thinking and doing that." When you limit yourself, that is when you stop living. Life is more than just watching television, eating, working, paying bills, and doing the same routine for 5-6 days straight and only enjoy yourself on Saturday or Sunday. When the fountain of Youth leaves you mentally, you start to go down hill into a depression and your life becomes boring. You can still be responsible and have fun while connecting with the people of all ages.

Eye still play video games, box, wrestle with the Youth....Eye still play basketball and football with the Youth....Eye still link up with brothers and throw parties for the Youth etc,etc....Eye still link up with those who are older and just hang out, talk, shoot pool and go to social events. Eye still dance and sing to old school and new school music. Eye still uplift and teach my people, etc,etc...Eye still joke around with the elders. Eye can adapt to anyone of any age and connect on a common ground. Age is only an illusion while most older people use their age as an excuse to stop living. We are still the Fountain of Youth and it never leaves us....you was just convinced that it left.

Stop being so angry and acting like something is stuck up your ass, and just live. Stop letting your jobs or your career justify who you are. That stress will only make you an asshole and a trained robot, who is letting life pass you by. Loosing up sometimes and smile or laugh a bit. Run and jump at the playground sometimes, care free...LIVE!!! Stop worrying what people think of you and what the people in your circle may think...Just Live...be you!

"MIND SEX"

"Don't ever think that you can keep a woman secured by only sexing her physically and providing for her."

"Tell that woman what she needs to know rather than what she wants to know. Let your words vibrate her mind and send chills up her spine to stop her train of thought. Give her what she never had before and say what she never heard before. Melt her emotions with fire and cool her down with ice cold love."

"The more you desire, the easier you will fall in love...The more you love, the less you will desire....so never desire to fall in love because love has no desire because it is already planted there, waiting to be nurtured and taken care of, for it to grow. Love is a growing blossoming flower and desires nothing but fresh fruit that needs to be picked and eaten before they rot....then its gone."

"A queen can have a orgasm way before you enter her universe. She absorbs every deep intellectual energy from a man's eye contact with her, from his words, and the way he gently touches her outer temple. She begins to moisten as you connect with her soul and it is happening right before you. So when you finally enter her universe, you wont experience her orgasm, but rather u will experience her big bang theory."

"A lot of people pretend to not want Love or their too afraid to obtain it, only because One day, they might loose it. No matter what the reason is...never leave this earth without experiencing its greatest gift...("Love")...it is worth every second of it."

"Respect the woman whether she Respects herself or not.....It is best for you to walk away or dismiss her before you find yourself disrespecting her. Your words has the ability to uplift her or destroy her 4ever."

    You know, sometimes Eye will just sit back and take a glance at the world. Sometimes Eye feel so alone that no one even really innerstands me. It's like everyone is out to satisfy themselves with their own greed and selfish desires. A lot of hate, love and chaos is going on all at the same time. Eye don't know what it is but it seems that my mind and spirit leaves my body sometimes as Eye glance at the world from a different realm. Is love temporary on earth? Is certain people, that you think loves you, pretending with you and is putting on a staged act, just to satisfy themselves? My mind wonders about these things because people tend to treat you differently when you are not stimulating them the way they want you to. They will ask you "What is wrong?", "Why are you acting different?", or "You changed.".....Then they separate themselves from you and they will find the next person to stimulate them.

    Fighting, Wars, Politics, etc ,etc....A man is never satisfied until he is satisfied with himself. What do you really want? That is the question. Give the man the whole world and he will be in search of another world. Eye sit and take a glance at the world and see that Man wants the weather to be the way he wants it. Sometimes Eye feel that The Most High and the Creator of all things should have never gave Man the authority on earth when he has an unstable spirit.

"As Eye sit back and glance at the world"

A beautiful world, Eye may add......the world is kind of similar to an insecure woman who has no confidence in herself and do not think she is beautiful, when in actuality, she is one of the most beautiful women that you will ever see. Maybe we don't value our world anymore....maybe we have lost sight on what we really have. We are so worried about profits where we are so loud that we are drowning out all the prophets. The fruits of the land has been mimicked and cloned. The gold and diamonds of this land has been mocked and made as replicas. Where do we find the originals? We must leave this earth mentally and spiritually, and take a glance from the outside to evaluate. Then we can come back into our physical forms and clean up the mess we have made.

"Not all those who wander, are lost."

"To believe in something and not live it, is dishonest."

Faith

Eye think a lot about faith and Eye evaluate everyone's beliefs. Some people live by what they believe, and some don't. For those that don't....they believe anyway. So this theory came to me about what faith really means and Eye see why people like to argue and debate on who's right or wrong, even when their beliefs are proven to be false. This goes for any kind of beliefs, even goals that we set for ourselves or the faith that we put in some people to be like we want them to be.

"Having faith that something is true, does not make it true. Having Faith does not make it probably true. Having faith has no bearing on truth whatsoever. Having faith simply means you will believe it whether it is true or not."

PSALMS OF THE YOUNG LOVE, PAIN, & CURIOSITY

-Poetry by Goldyn Akachi...the Youth years

"If Eye Die 2night"

Open my eyelids and look deeply in my eyes,
See my pain and suffering through the years Eye despised.
As you can see, my tears have stopped flowing,
close your eyes to see my soul,
and picture my soul glowing.
Should Eye die before my time,
Eye would remember what was mine.
Everyone who REALLY loved me would feel my presence, don't fear,
the end is near, so don't you shed a tear.
My enemies will crumble,
as the thunder in the sky rumbles.
If Eye die 2night,
Eye was laid,
Eye did not tumble.

"Strong Woman"

- 4 you

Tears from your eyes are never seen.
You heart is so pure,
if you know what Eye mean.
Independent and your authentic style is a blessing,
while men nonchalant attitudes, never has you stressing.
He can't bring you down
because your up and out.
Keeping your head up
is what this is about.
You bring me 2 a climax without sex,
Your passion is so deep
it digs deeper inside of my chest.
Your not like others, you lead and not follow,
words from your lips are always solid and never hollow.
And if your taken 2day
Eye will find a strong woman like you....
2morrow!!

"The Weakness In A Man's Eyes"

A woman's beautiful smile,
A hungry and abandoned child.

*-knowing a woman's needs
but cannot fulfilled them.-*

Neglect from mother and father.
Staring at his reflection, makes him bothered.

*-unstable emotions of his soul and faith
makes him change in grief.-*

The one whom he trusted and loved, just dies.
And after that........
You can see the weakness the Man's eyes.

"Wonder Woman"

-4 Anna w/love

The Universe aligned you with me for a reason.
If you weren't there at that time, Eye wouldn't be breathing.(as of now)
Girlfriend, Eye am not sure,
but that's what you call it.
Not putting to much in this relationship,
so Eye guess we could never spoil it.
Eye treat you so unfair, but your still there,
and having my affairs makes you kind of aware.
You let me live my life, so Eye can't complain.
Eye can only count on you to keep me dry,
every time it rains.
My love 4 you is unpredictable and unconditionally,
and Eye always think to myself that 1 day....
you'll leave me eventually.
Sometimes Eye really love you,
and sometimes Eye really hat you,
but Eye always wonder.....
Why do Eye keep thinking of you?

"The Sun Didn't Rise This Morning"

When my brother died last night.....
                        the Sun didn't rise.

When my mother cried last night.....
                        the Sun didn't rise.

When my parents got divorced.....
                        the Sun didn't rise.

Eye think Eye am wrong and heartless,
and when Eye awakened this morning,
      there was total darkness.

"Private Eye"

Everyone has a private eye,
Their in disguise and you wonder why.
Watching your every move and constant step,
paranoid and distracted, you'll think you need help.
Watch what you do, it will haunt you later,
and everything you do now, you'll eventually see it later.
When you ask me, "Where's my private eye?
Eye sit and smile, because,
all along....your Private Eye is your own child!!!

"A Shining Star Within"

-4 Starleena

Wounded with a broken heart,
Not looking for brighter days beyond and after the dark.
Independent and strong,
so why do you welcome defeat?
Sometimes it may feel like you have fell,
but you really landed on your feet.
Your heart can be fixed if your heart is pure,
don't look 4 love, let love find you until your sure.
You get out what you put in,
Eye see and Eye think you should look within yourself,
and see the Shining Star Within.

"The Most Beautiful Thing To See"

-The Sunrise-

The Sunrise is the most beautiful thing to see.
A new day, a new life, and a new breed.
A new light has overcome the darkness of there.
A child's scare is no longer aware.
So lift your voice and sing,
and witness
2 see the most beautiful thing.

-The Children of the Sun has risen-

"Days Goes By"

-4 Sparkle

Eye would cherish this day.....
but days goes by.

Eye would make a change 2day.....
but days goes by.

Bye, there goes days.
All was done and said,
just went astray.

Eye would love you 2day.....
but days goes by.

Real love is 4ever

and Eye can't say it 2day.....
cause days go by.

BYE!!!

"Waiting 4 Death"

A death wish contains no strings attached.
The Sorrow it brings, u can't even hold it back.
Wondering what's next in your days ahead.
Your life is like a dream or mirage that rest in your head.
Your happiness has a time limit,
and sometimes it makes you timid.
It seems like there's nothing in this world to offer you.
The Sun is shining, your free and blessed, but you still feel blue.
Nothing distracts you....Love or even an enemies threat,
because your so caught up, anxiously waiting for death.

"The Heart Wants What The Heart Wants"

Eye was happy with *YOU*, then *SHE* came along.
The Eye saw *HER* and then *SHE* moved along.

Eye fell in love with *HER*, but Eye still had love for *YOU*.
Then *SHE* came and *HER* loved felt true.

Eye still love *YOU*, but *HER* and *SHE* feels new and better....
but no matter however, *YOU* can be with me whenever.

Now *SHE* is getting jealous of *HER*,
And that makes me sick of *SHE*.
There's only one me,
but y'all are equal to three.

Now *SHE* is gone again and it's just *YOU* and *HER*.
Now *HER* always wants the last word.
HER wants me to herself or herself is leaving,
but Eye told *HER* about the situation at first, so that's not a good enough reason.

So now it's just *YOU* and me standing with pride and flaunt.
You stood by my side and trusted my heart of what it really wants.
                                             And that's *YOU*.....

So now *YOU* tell me that your fed up and that your heart can't take no more....
and you walk away with my heart in your hands as Eye lay astray.

"GOLDYNCHILE"

-The meaning behind the alias-

G – Genuine
O – Open
L – Loyal
D – Determined
Y – Yearning
N – Nice
C – Cunning
H – Honorable
I – Intelligent
L – Lovable
E – Energetic

by: Kourtney

"Eye Must Say Goodbye"

- 2 Shameika

Eye thank Cupid for bringing you to me,
you cured my blindness of love
and you made me see.

When Eye fell in love with you,
Eye knew it was a lifetime of pain.
We always loved the sunny days,
but could never stand the rain.

My heart can't take no more,
you left me with grief.
Eye trusted you to every extinct,
now you left me with disbelief.

Sometimes Eye want you,
Sometimes Eye don't,
If Eye am not sure,
that means Eye don't.

Eye cannot confuse my heart,
so Eye have to walk away.
Never no more will you see me,
not 2morrow
and sure not 2day.

So don't call
and don't you try,
Eye have 2 move on.....

So Eye Must Say Goodbye!!!

"UNTITLED"

How can you move forward when you are looking behind?

How can you see when your mind is blind?

You are yearning for a need that doesn't really matter.

Love and respect yourself, if not, be prepared for the disaster.

Don't risk a lifetime of something for a temporary thing.

It seems great, the feeling is great, but what does it really bring?

Patience is the key to unlock all stored questions.

And Impatience will be your downfall of all blessings.

What you really want may come in a way that you don't want.

Don't push it away, listen and learn, if not, it will taunt.

Be good to your mind by opening & elevating it...not your heart.

Your heart is not honest, it is filled with so many emotions and personalities.
So be smart!!!

"Jealous Whispers"

What are those noises when Eye walk by?
What was said and done, when Eye said, "Bye"?
When Eye looked up, you looked away.
Ypu watched me like you had something to say.
Eye found out things about me that Eye didn't even much know.
As false as it is, someone was there to start the show.

Now they look at me differently....
      from those jealous whispers.
Now they are seeing me differently....
      from those jealous whispers.

Why don't these whispers become clearer?
Is it because Eye am getting nearer?
Jealous whispers really do not bother me,
because Jealous Whispers on whispers Jealousy.

> **Everybody isn't your friend.**
>
> Just because they hang around you and laugh with you doesn't mean they are your friend. People pretend well. At the end of the day, real situations expose fake people, so pay attention.

"The Rain"

The rain makes me drowsy at times.
It makes me think of why the Sun didn't shine.
Rain brings me pain that's contained,
but the contained pain always feel the same.

They say that the rain cleanses the earth of its sins,
but some hate it when it rains because they can't begin.
The flows down like the blood in your veins,
and it's weird how rain became it's name.

Rain is a blessing from the Higher Power above.
By going through the rain, you'll appreciate the Sun above.
Rain is similar to the hard work that you do,
but you don't want to do it....true.
After the hard work and rain,
there will be sunshine and rewards,
and no more pain or rain to obtain.

"Is This Cupid's Blessing?"
-2 my future Goddess Queen Dominique who Eye spoke into existance

Eye use to walk with my head down,
because my love for self and others was now gone.
My smiles were turned to frowns,
so Eye moaned and groaned.

Now you came along and made me smile,
you gave this King what Eye looked for, for a while.
Eye know it's so sudden but Eye feel that Eye love you.
And when our souls touched,
Eye couldn't imagine myself without you.

When you look at me, it makes me.......
Just like that, Eye am lost for words.
When Eye look at you,
Eye see an angel in my world.

Eye know it's not lust,
or another love lesson,
because Eye feel it in my heart.

Eye know Cupid is not real and it's just another symbolism of Love,
but why does it feel that someone just shot me in my heart with an arrow?
Eye love the feeling!!!

"In2 My Creation"

Who expected the unexpected,
with plenty power,
not a coward.
A gifted mind with self dignity,
higher than any tower.

A lyrical land mind suggested,
A poet, you know it,
my candle burns eternally,
so you can't blow it...
so Eye will show it.

A man of steel who doesn't welcome defeat.
Don't hate me because we are One,
and self-hate only makes you weak.

(LEO)

Eye conquer and is a ruler of all situations,
so be very careful of what you do,
when you step **In2 My Creation**.

"Even when they speak down on me, they speak highly of me."

"Outlaw"
                                          -2 Jakita

A beautiful young Princess with lots to offer.
Neglected from mother and beaten by father.
Outcast from family, left on her own.
A star was born so she can't fall or go wrong.
She makes a young Prince feel like a King when she is in his arms.
That night that we experienced our first kiss, you felt like my lucky charm.
Off into the sunset you went and left me thinking,
wondering if you are okay, and Eye am still thinking.
The remembrance of you was the sparkling diamonds in your eyes,
Hoping to see it again right before the sunrise.
Until we meet again, you will always be in my heart,
and how can we end this, for we never had a chance to start.

-We were only 13yrs old when we kissed and this is the last image in my mind that Eye have of you. Eye am sure that you have grown up into a Beautiful Queen-

"Living Just 2 Die"

After Life, there's death,
    and perhaps, a better life.

2 strive for that better life,
    you must live before
  you die, right?

You cannot die just to live,
    some just live to die
to get that constant thrill.

So your will to live, is okay,
    but you have no choice....

You must die!!!

"No One Really Cares"

*Lonely nights filled with depression,
who;s there to comfort me with suggestions?
My only friend is my pain,
devastation of the rain,
makes me insane.
They say that they care,
but their words tickle my heart,
that makes me unaware.
Eye try to care for others,
but as long as their happy,
Eye am just another.
In the end Eye die alone.
A closed casket at my funeral,
and no ones in it.
Let me be alone, Eye swear...
Only when Eye die,
They assumed they cared.*

"Living Inside My Mind"

A place that's so beautiful and free.
No hatred or envy towards me.
My world contains no money,
anything you want and need, you have,
not even funny.
No sickness, sadness or worries,
and no liars or thieves who told stories.
In my mind, Eye have the perfect woman with me.
She worships me, and Eye worship her.
The Most High looks highly upon us, which is our president,
and paradise is our residence.

Eye am so in peace when Eye am **Living Inside My Mind**.

"Outcast"

-2 me

Eye shall distant myself from you,
because you don't understand what Eye have been through.
Judge me, love me, then hug me....
that doesn't make sense to me.

Blood and water runs in the same direction,
but you never should have judge or condemn me.

Eye see things the way The Most High blesses me to see things.
That's why Eye strive alone and take full responsibilities,
of what life brings.

Eye love me and Eye feel uncomfortable loving you,
because if your love was true in return,
you wouldn't abandon that love when Eye needed you.

Eye cry alone and Eye will die alone.

Eye am an Outcast,
and Eye feel more comfortable being alone.

"Game Over"

Why explain the game, people not listening,
the fake recognizing the real, but they still bullshitting.
Explain to me, nah Eye am going to explain to you,
of how the game is just an illusion and an image,
that some people find not true.
If you are real, Eye am going to put you through a test.
Do you hold back what you want to say,
or do you get that stress off your chest?

Why explain the game, people not listening,
the real recognizing the fake, but they still bullshitting.
Watch who you spit your knowledge to,
because in the long run that knowledge that you spitting,
will soon be used against you.
The rules of the game remains the same,
but the game seem strange,
and you might find it hard to understand.

Why explain the game, people not listening.
The real feel what Eye am saying,
but the fake will find it hard to understand what Eye am spitting.
The game consist of........excuse me!
Didn't Eye mention before?......Game Over!!!

-FREEDOM OF THE MIND IS A PEACE OF MIND-

"A person's actions will tell you everything you need to know. Don't try to paint a different picture."

"Eye knew Eye was growing mentally and spiritually when Eye started telling people "Let me help you", rather than saying "Eye will pray for you."

Some of the most important conversations that will have an impact on our child's life, is sometimes held at the dinner table. We must sit and converse with our kids at times instead of talking at them all the time. Just sit and really listen to them...make an connection and vibe with them. They will Respect you more and it will be easy for them to be honest and be willing to open up to you.

Most of us have gotten to a point where we are not even interested in our own children or the Youth around us. Some are far more wiser than some adults. Let's break that chain of not sitting around eating with our children. Never get too busy where you ignoring the most precious things in life.

Please....Eye want you guys to really, really, Eye mean really try to innerstand this. Take your time and reevaluate everything about yourself and how you really feel about yourself. Think...Are Your actions based off your insecurities or confidence of what you really think of yourself?

"We kill flowers because we think their beautiful."

"We kill ourselves because we think we are not"

Who has the gun pointing at you? Who's finger is really on the trigger? Is their face clear enough for you?

When you see something beautiful in someone, tell them. It may take seconds to say, but for them, it could last a life time.

Be Weird. Be Random. Be Who You Are. Because You Never Know Who Would Love The Person You Hide.

"Never trade in your positive morality, to follow a negative trend, just to feel loved or accepted."

"You don't find your worth in a man. You find your worth within yourself and then find a man who's worthy of you. Remember that."

Sex has become so meaningless to most single and unmarried women. At the same time, most Men think the sex that they get from these same women, means something..... and that's why they become so attached to these women that don't even want them in the way he thinks she does.

Some women have been hurt and used so much that they are using Men the same way that Men uses them. It's like Karma in motion. The scary part about this is that her womb has the power to hurt and deceive any Man who catches feelings for her.

A woman is most dangerous when she has been hurt and disappointed several times by all the men in her life. Vengeance will always be set in her heart and it's up to her free-will to act on it.

Until that woman finds her true worth, you better not touch a broken woman because she will burn you.

Real Friendship
9 times out of 10, most of you have so-called friends that say only good things to your face and talk so badly about you behind your back. Y'all just got attached to one another through the years, that's all.

That's why it is better to have enemies than friends now a

days...at least your enemy will let you know how they really feel about you and you know where they stand. Some men are emotional and emasculated so they catch feelings when another man tell them about themselves and they will stop talking to you.....and some females are not use to their female friends being honest with them because they really envy one another.

True friends will hurt your feelings sometimes by telling you what you need to hear about yourself to your face.

"True Friends say good things behind your back and say bad things to your face."

You know what? Sometimes Eye really get frustrated and Eye feel that Eye just need to get away from everyone. It's like when Eye experience a new view or a new experience, it relaxes me and calms me down. Eye so love the feeling. This feeling made me come up with this logic.......

Stress, anger, bitterness and negativity in a person is most of the times cause by being in one place too long and seeing and doing the same things everyday. Maybe you need to meet different kinds of people and see to experience many different beautiful places to finally free your mind.

Sometimes you may have to step away from the same kind of negative friends or social media friends that you have who are always talking about negativity and just add different kinds of people with a different mindset and energies into your life. Most people don't really innerstand certain things completely because they have never been anywhere so they are only thinking inside of a box. Keep expanding your horizon....that's the only way to grow and obtain wisdom over deceitful emotions.

> TRAVEL.
> AS MUCH AS YOU CAN.
> AS ~~FAR~~ AS YOU CAN.
> AS LONG AS YOU CAN.
> LIFE'S NOT MEANT TO BE
> LIVED IN ONE
> PLACE.

Being Negative

Negative thinking is One of the most pervasive and universal problems of human kind. If you are a negative thinker, you may not realize the power this habit has over your life. People will always feel your negative vibes & energy, no matter where you go or get involved in.

Try meditating on this so it can help release those negative energies...Just think about ways in which you are habitually negative in your thoughts or speech.

For one full day, refrain from saying or thinking anything negative. Note when you had to make negative or sarcastic comments or had negative thoughts about someone or something...(Hmm be honest with yourself) As you witness your negative thoughts arise, you will be amazed at the negativity in your mind.

Be gentle with yourself and simply note to the negativity.

Don't punish yourself for it. Have a few laughs at how negative and foolish your mind can be. Start to begin to be more positive and supportive in your thoughts and words.

How you think, determines your reality. If your first thought is to see the World darkly, you are going to live in a dark World. If your habit is to zoom in on what is wrong with a person, an idea or thing, this World is not going to be a satisfying place for you. You may think you are being realistic, intelligent or discriminating, but you are actually stuck with a warped view of the World. Negative thinking is bad for your health, your relationships, and your spiritual life. You will continue to push your love ones away.

Eye avoid & ignore negative people....never feed into them or welcome their spirits in.....

People...we are going to have to add some spontaneous things in our lives rather than just going to work and coming home. Many people just wait for the weekend to do things. So you tell me that you actually live 2 days out of a week? That's why many of us have health problems because our bodies get sick from the same sitting routine. Our melanin selves are not built and designed that way. We need to stay active and creating. We have trained ourselves to be robots and sheep to the system. Learn to enjoy yourselves everyday. Surprise yourself, your kids, or the One you are with and stop being so predictable. Watch less of the idiot Box(T.V.) and experience this beautiful World and its people. Its okay to live the safe and responsible life by doing the same thing everyday, Eye am not knocking you.....but sometimes that woman or Man, or even your kids want to just be rebellious to the system and just get up and do something out of the ordinary....Just Live baby!!! or you will grow into a miserable grump.

Marriages & Serious Relationships

Be careful whose shoulders you cry on.

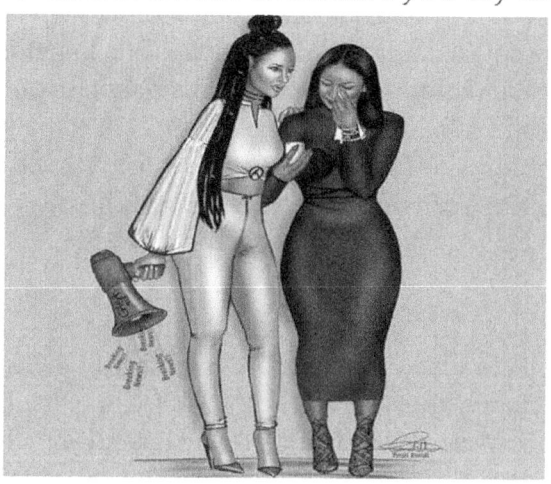

If you are in a serious relationship and especially if you are married, please keep people out of your business. Sometimes you have to definitely keep your family members out of your business as well. Tell them just the basics of what you think they should know. Just keep them gossiping & guessing. Sometimes your own family members can envy your relationships and your marriage. Some parents sometimes feel that they should come first before your spouse, but they are wrong. Your husband or your wife must come first no matter what.

If you don't trust your spouse, then y'all shouldn't be together. You must satisfy each other before you try to satisfy other people in your family or friends. Sometimes your parents can envy your spouse because they do not have that marriage, love relationship, so they try their best to separate y'all and turn y'all against each other. Please, be careful on what kind of energies you take in from these people because you might end up bringing those same negative energies into your own home and it will cause problems. Even in the scriptures it says that a Man & Woman shall leave their mother and Father and become One flesh in unity. So please innerstand how important and powerful your marriage is. Let no Man or Woman come between you two.

Also Stop feeding into negativity and drama caused by these single, bitter, and miserable people, for they love starting drama because it satisfies them. Your main Focus should be on your spouse and building up a strong Foundation in your own home and if others want to support & respect it, so be it....if not, keep building. If your family and friends don't respect your spouse, then they really don't respect you. So, like Eye said before, keep envious people out of your business.

Listen closely...Eye am about to give y'all the game. Those who are in relationships or whatever the case may be. If you are the one who is insecure or always worried about someone cheating on you, then you need to stop. Jealous & envy is a dangerous thing and also bad for your health. If that person is with you, their with you...just do what you suppose to be doing. You see, a lot of you are not doing what your suppose to be doing and that's why you get so insecure when your partner's attention goes somewhere else. But Peep this...a person is going to cheat regardless if you nag & spy on that person or not. It's nothing you can do about it. You just have to know who you are with and hopefully their the right one for you. Have confidence in yourself and your relationship, because all that worrying and stressing about other people trying to steal your partner is foolish. People are going to always admire and find the person that your with attractive no matter where you go. It's totally different when someone is disrespecting you purposely, trying to steal what you have. But don't be so much worried about who want the person that you are with, just take care of your business. Your relationships will be so much less stressful...trust me. Insecurities & jealousy destroys relationships and pushes your partner away mentally & physically. That fire y'all have will burn out & your relationship will become like a prison, dull & boring. How can a person make someone be faithful when they don't want to? That's not realistic...you will stress yourself into having a nervous breakdown or having a heart-attack trying to do that. Stress causes you to age quickly.

Progress & Self Elevation

Eye know Eye am not the only one who feels like this sometimes and Eye know some of you still feel this way...but hey...it's time to move on and be more productive with our time. If that person or people next to you won't get up and walk with you, don't be afraid to get up and walk alone. Sometimes you have to do that and then if they are really down for you, they will rise up, wise up and catch up to you.

All it takes is that one step forward....the past is the past...pick ya head up and walk forward.

Don't force so much knowledge unto people where you forget how to engage with them. Sometimes you have to be a great listener to really innerstand how they think and where they are coming from. Then you can make a connection and build from there.

Looking into the eyes of the Youth, you can learn something precious that will always get you through whatever your going through. Don't influence and destroy them with your worldly desires and images of what they should grow up to look like and chase after.

(This is what you tell those people when they say you have changed or acting funny)

"Eye don't hate you, it's just that we were going in two different directions. Eye was ready to live and you was willing to die. Eye was ready to wake up and you was too comfortable sleeping. Eye wanted to walk with the Giants but rather you chose to stay crawling with the ants. This world is too big for me to stay idle in a box with you, having the same mindset and outlook on life..."

Love ones and true friends encourages you and ride with you to higher elevations in life, not those who are afraid of heights. Enjoy the new transition in your lives..

Share the wisdom you recieve. Knowledge is power, empower those around you.

We are linked to so much information and knowledge that being ignorant is a choice. Some spend hours and hours everyday, seeking to be entertained by pornography, music videos, violence, or just being hateful and negative on other people's social media pages and they wonder why they don't innerstand and comprehend real issues. That same energy that you put in searching for foolishness, use that same energy to research and educate yourself. Nothing wrong with having fun, but keep a healthy balance.

And some people keep wondering why their lives keep going in circles. Still going through the same drama with the same people. You want real change....change your surroundings, because obviously these people are not making your life no better than what it is.

Teach your kids to have common sense and not to believe everything their told, just because an adult tell them something. Some...well maybe a lot of these adults these days are very ignorant, immature & very shallow. So educate yourself, because if you are dumb as a box of rocks, then your kids will be just as dumb as a box of rocks as well.

"The reason why people give up so fast is because they tend to look at how far they still have to go, instead of how far they have come."

-The Solution to this is to live for and through the moment.-

There is a quote by Billie Holiday that says.....

"You've got to have something to eat and a little love in your life before you can hold still for any damn body's sermon on how to behave."

This quote is basically saying that when other people decide to try to discipline others or preach to others, make sure that the person you are talking to is not desperately in need of something. How can anyone sit still and listen to you when they are worried about where their next meal is coming from. Also some people might be dealing with some serious demons where they have so much hate in their heart, where they are always thinking about taking their anger out on everyone they see. A person can look you dead in your eyes and still not here a thing that you are saying. So make sure you can connect with them physically before you try to connect with them mentally.

Another quote that stood out to me was by the singer Jimi Hendrix.

"When the power of love overcomes the love for power, the world will know peace."

"The Emblem that Eye have in my hand and around my neck is called the "SANKOFA BIRD". Sankofa is a word in the Twi language of Ghana that translates as "Go back and get it" (san - to return; ko - to go; fa - to fetch, to seek and take) and also refers to the Asante Adinkra symbol represented either by a bird with its head turned backwards taking an egg off its back, or as a stylist heart shape. Sankofa is often associated with the proverb, "Se wo were fi na wosankofa a yenkyi," which translates as: "It is not wrong to go back for that which you have forgotten."

      The Sankofa Bird reminds us to always seek our original roots. Also to reflect on our past to build a successful future. How can we know where we are going if we don't know where we came from. Just like a conversation....how can you dig what Eye am saying if you don't know where Eye am coming from. Always embrace your many cultures and your roots, no matter what race you are....

"Promote what you love RATHER than bashing what you hate"

Sometimes you may have to respond quickly to the negative experiences by creating even greater positive experiences. Remember, we will always see and go through negative situations.....we cannot run from it, but we can embrace it a point it is not effecting our will to conquer it with positive productivity. Love conquers all. Expose the problems with solutions. A person is at their strongest when they are going to war to protect and fight for what they truly love.

Deception

-Everything that glitters ain't Gold-

Smooth Conscious words are easy to put 2gether and powerful conscious symbols and clothes are easy to wear, but when it comes to actually living it, now that's the hard part. That's when you see who that person actually is.

Eye see a lot of sisters and brothers who are really good with words and knowledge, but do not have any wisdom to put things into action. Most of these women say they are so conscious but continually to let these sorry beta males get them pregnant without a real commitment. They are continuing to do things backwards. How can you become so conscious and create a life, but have no real attachments or unity to the Man when both male and female represents the ankh(unity). All we doing is faking and disrespecting our Ancestors and the natural order of things. We are only drawing negative energy and low vibrations to us. We keep repeating the same cycle that tearing down our culture...and we continue to praise it and to see nothing wrong with what we are doing.

Don't be fooled and deceived by the hype of these people that you praise and follow when their own life does not reflect what they say.

*"Just because you say "F*ck the system" or whatever, doesn't make you a Revolutionary."*

"Just because you get killed by the system that you claim to go against doesn't make you a Revolutionary."

"Just because you speak like your conscious or a person with intelligence, and put on a costume doesn't make you what you say you are."

You have to practice what you preach....you have to take your own advice before you expect someone to take in that same advice you give them. Walk in that same LIGHT that you hold up. Don't be quick to put people on pedestals of what they say regardless of what you see them do physically. There is a teacher for every student, some people have different effects on different people.

**THAT MOMENT WHEN A WOMAN LOVES
AND ADMIRES A MAN'S SPIRIT**

GOLDYN AKACHI

**WITHOUT LOOKING AT HIM SEXUALLY
OR WANTING TO DATE HIM**

      Eye think every woman on earth NEEDS a real Masculine Man in their life to reach & connect with them mentally & spiritually. That Man doesn't even have to be her lover or date him....she just need that Male figure to relate & open up to, so she can exhale without being criticize or used for something. Women mature faster than Men, believe it or not....because the woman carries life & nurtures it. Eye to tend to connect with a lot of women, more than Eye do with Men. Not because Eye don't get along with Men, because Eye do, just not as much as Eye do with women. Eye know how to attract & connect with the mind of a woman & feed her spiritually. Eye know the importance she is to our lives. So never THINK that its a sexual thing or that Eye want them in a physical way. Eye have introduce brothers to women that Eye know and hooked them up, but at the same time, these same brothers turned on me. Some have gotten jealous or had this envy towards me because they see that these women & Men really appreciate what Eye do and the connection that we have. Don't get it twisted, Eye have many brothers as friends who see Eye to Eye with me & they innerstand the concept.

You cannot be me and Eye cannot be you...but the solution is to have more Men being able to stimulate these women minds like they need to be stimulated. Step away from the television and your homeys sometimes and have some deep talks with these women. Just listen to them. Open her mind up from time to time. Don't talk down on other brothers just to make yourself look good in her eyes or to feel better about yourself. These brothers are not trying to trick and deceive women to get them in the bed..... so what Eye do is not for attention or to flatter them. These are not my fans....Some people just don't know what true friendship is and what it is to be loyal to someone who loves you without wanted anything from you. Trust me, Eye see and hear everything and it always comes back to me, so Eye just kick the dust off my feet and keep moving. A Man will always envy another Man before a Woman does.

So these brothers shouldn't let other Men intimidate them. Eye just try to Master everything Eye seek and learn, especially about Women. Eye don't mind giving you the Knowledge. Its up to you to obtain the Wisdom, to be able to put it into action.

The Most High gives us all gifts & talents. Trust me, these women know when you are pretending, they feel it inside....Its a spiritual vibration that will always catch their attention in their minds. Don't be too comfortable when you have her physically, because you May never have her mentally and spiritually....& best believe that she will always find that connection to stimulate her mind in someone else. Every Woman needs this kind of Man in her life, no matter who he is. So don't make this about the brothers who are the ones stimulating them, cause its not, they cannot help who they are. Eye will always keep the balance on my side. How about you?

Now Eye innerstand the concept of why there are a few male Lions, walking around with a lot of female Lions.

"Respond quickly to the negative experiences by creating even greater positive experiences."

Sometimes people act like it's just them against the world but it's really just them against themselves. This is the reality that everyone is afraid of and do not want to accept. Some people get so flattered of themselves when they think everyone is hating on them. It's like they feed for it.

You know, It comes a point in time where we need to upgrade our friends......

> I need more spiritual friends.
> More higher conscious ones.
> The use of common sense ones.
> More open-minded ones.
> That know thyself ones.
> Leaves their ego at the door ones.
> The free-spirit ones.
> You know, the adventurous ones.
> That's also into nature ones.
> That can have a good conversation ones.

This would be so nice to have.

"Stay In Your Own Lane"

"Never, ever be so envious and admire someone else blessing or accomplishments so much, that you start to feel that you have to do exactly what they did to be successful. Sometimes what is best for them is not really best for you. We all have different paths to take and different obstacles to face that will better and strengthen us in the long run and we will show more appreciation to our accomplishment.

Just because it took them a short while to get where they are going, doesn't mean that it will happen so quickly for you. Maybe your reward will be bigger if you just wither the storm, meaning that sometimes we don't get what we want as of now because we are not mentally ready and what we wish for as of now will destroy us or make us a bad individual. If we spend more time focusing on ourselves rather than what others are doing, then we will probably put the effort we need to put in our own hustle.

There is a season for everything....just stay in your own lane and you will be surprised what awaits you in the long run. It may even come in a wink of an eye, by being right in front of you...Blessings come in all shapes and sizes and The Most High knows what you can handle as of now, if you are right within. A fool is willing to be in a rush to gain the whole world but at the same time the fool will loose everything that he or she prospers because their mindset and spirit is so foul. There is no such thing as luck......it's about being in the right place at the right time, rising to the occasion, and not being so afraid or lazy to not put in the effort or hard work to achieve what you set your mind to.

Everything circulates in the Universe, if you missed what you wanted this time or made a few mistakes....then you pick yourself up and try again. You only fail when you STOP trying. Success requires no time limit...control the time and your own destiny...better yet, STAY IN YOUR OWN LANE.

"Before you run your mouth on someone, run by a mirror and discuss what you see."

"If you LOVE yourself, you LOVE others. If you HATE yourself, you HATE others. In relationship with others, it is only YOU mirrored." -OSHO

You might want to look twice the next time you LOOK INTO THE MIRROR....

"Misery & Hate is nothing and has no power without your company." -Goldyn Akachi

Always pay attention to those who always have something negative to say or post about someone. That should tell you who they really are inside.

Remember, before you find something to die for...you better make sure you find something TO LIVE FOR. That way, people will remember and mourn you 4ever rather than just that cause of that moment.

That's more important.....THINK! When Eye am done living for myself, my family, my friends...then Eye won't mind physically dying for them, because Eye will spiritually live forever in the minds of those Eye touched and shined the Light on.

> ## Sometimes people try to destroy you, precisely because they recognize your power - not because they don't see it, but because they see it and they don't want it to exist.

If a person of the past claims that they know me....they are a liar...and if Eye don't converse or associate with them now mentally or physically....then they surely don't know who Eye am and they know nothing about me. Eye elevate everyday...the past is dead, it has no POWER if it is not used in the present.

EYE SEE YOU!!!

To Love & To Be Loved....To Respect & To be Respected.....All you have to do is to accept, Love & Respect yourself...that is the key to happiness.....Look to the Universe (the Heavens) & be thankful for the skin that you are in, regardless of the shade of color. It's your choice and responsibility of what you decide to do in that flesh that was given to you. Are you going to follow the crowd, or is you going to be the one who moves the crowd? Love yourself, your people, and those who show you that they love or respect you. No one is guilty of an act of cultural past until they are proven guilty in the present. Let a person show you who they are before you condemn them. People cannot represent an individual, but rather an individual can represent a People."
*What's in the dark must come to the LIGHT...Expose the evil, so the Good can rest.

-EYE DON'T THROW SHADE, EYE SHED LIGHT-

-FREEDOM OF THE MIND, IS A PEACE OF MIND-

Dedicated to my big brother Louis Miller.

Eye did it!!!

May your body rest in peace while your spirit lives forever.

Made in the USA
Middletown, DE
07 May 2023